Christian Caregiving

a Way of Life

KENNETH C. HAUGK

STEPHEN MINISTRIES • St. Louis, Missouri

I0962877

Christian Caregiving—a Way of Life

ISBN: 978-1-930445-30-7

Library of Congress Control Number: 2013933638

Printed in the U.S.A.

14
2

To Joan, Charity, and Amity,
who continue to teach and show me
by their words and actions
what Christian caregiving is all about

Contents

Foreword

I first read *Christian Caregiving—a Way of Life* more than two decades ago. I was training to become a Stephen Minister along with 21 other members of a church in Phoenix, Arizona. *Christian Caregiving* laid the Christ-centered foundation for the one-to-one caring ministry we would provide to hurting people in our congregation and community.

Several years later, I read it again on a flight to St. Louis for a job interview with Stephen Ministries. I was excited not only about the possibility of joining the staff of an organization that empowers high-quality ministry in thousands of congregations but also about meeting Dr. Kenneth Haugk, founder and executive director of Stephen Ministries. That interview began a relationship that I still enjoy and value today.

A few years later, I read *Christian Caregiving* again—this time as a Stephen Leader at my church in St. Louis, when my pastor and I were co-teaching our congregation's first class of 19 Stephen Ministers. A decade later, many of them are still actively involved. In Phoenix, in St. Louis, or anywhere else, Christian caregiving truly becomes a way of life.

I read it again a few years ago when both of my children were in high school. I was teaching relational skills to our church youth group and wanted to help our teens incorporate some of the key concepts and skills into their own lives.

Every time I read *Christian Caregiving,* I rediscover why I like it so much: its down-to-earth practicality. In the author's own words, it's a "how-to manual" for caring and relating in distinctively Christian ways. Whether the subject is listening fully, relating to deep spiritual needs, sharing a blessing, building a prayer, or offering a cup of cold water, *Christian Caregiving* presents tangible ways we can be Christ to others every day.

Not just anyone could write this book. Ken Haugk has a Ph.D. in clinical psychology and practiced and taught psychotherapy for many years. An ordained clergyperson, he has served as both a parish pastor and seminary professor. His passion has always been "to equip God's people for the work of ministry." He draws on this background in *Christian Caregiving,* blending sound psychology with biblical theology and expressing it in words that everyone can understand and put into action.

Over the years, more than a half-million people have read this book as part of Stephen Minister training, hundreds of thousands as part of the *Christian Caregiving* course and many more on their own. I welcome you into this growing wave of *Christian Caregiving* readers who are making its Christ-centered principles and practices a way of life.

Joel P. Bretscher
Director of Communications
Stephen Ministries
St. Louis, Missouri

Preface

The purpose of this book is twofold: to describe what makes Christian caregiving distinctive and to explain how that distinctive caregiving can become a way of life for individual Christians. It is a resource for Christians who wonder, "What unique difference can my Christianity make in the caring and relating I do?"

Today's world needs Christians who care, but the distictiveness of Christian caring is frequently unrecognized and unarticulated, and consequently, never actualized. For this reason, I think we all could benefit from some frank discussion of *Christian* caregiving.

Christian Caregiving—a Way of Life is practical, a how-to manual. It deals with real-life issues in caring and relating. The Christian orientation informing this book is like that of C. S. Lewis's *Mere Christianity:* a grass-roots faith common to all Christians.

I write from the perspective that Christian caregivers need to be built up and affirmed, but not at the expense of the valuable contributions of psychology and other arts and sciences. The world needs all the caring it can get, from both psychology and theology.

I experienced great pleasure and satisfaction writing this book. As I wrote, the subject assumed greater meaning and urgency. I hope that you will be caught up in the vision of Christian caregiving and that you will be uplifted as well.

1

It's Not Easy

Looking at him, you would say, "What a fine, upstanding Christian!" You would be right; he is. Peter L. is 39, married, and the father of two—a daughter and a son. Although his church attendance was sporadic for several years when he was younger, Peter has been involved in church work throughout his life—serving on boards and committees, pitching in when there was work to be done, and taking part in his congregation's program of visitation to shut-ins and the hospitalized.

Yet he shrugs that off. "I just try to help out where I'm needed," he says. What about his volunteer work in the home for the mentally retarded? "Oh, that," says Peter, "Well, you know, that's not really connected with our church. I just go down there to show the kids how to make things out of wood." Ruefully, he shows a thumbnail turning black. "Last time I showed 'em how to hammer your thumb."

When asked about his faith, Peter is likely to hesitate. "I'm not really big on talking about my religion," he says. "I suppose that makes me less of a Christian. But I don't believe in pushing my faith down anyone's throat. Last year I went to New Orleans for our company's annual sales convention. After dinner three of us went for a walk and ran into a sidewalk preacher. You never heard such shouting, haranguing and wild predictions. It really turned me off. I was cringing inside. The two guys I was with were cracking jokes about the fellow and religion in general. I was really mad at the sidewalk preacher for being such an easy target, and I was angry with myself for lacking the guts and knowledge to defend my faith. I didn't want to defend him, because ranting and raving isn't what Christianity is all about. But I thought, *What if one of my friends asks me what it is all about? I don't think I can explain it.''*

Peter L. is by no means fictitious. He is a composite of you, me, and many others—old and young, women and men. What we have in common is Christianity and the difficulties we can experience in being distinctively Christian.

Every Christian will experience one or more of these difficulties at some time. We all fail despite our best attempts. In Paul's words, "All . . . fall short of the glory of God" (Rom. 3:23). Jesus Christ is the only person who never failed when he faced these difficulties. Each Christian will experience different difficulties, some more, others less. Only Christ had no difficulties being distinctively Christian.

I want to help you become comfortable with your shortcomings, but, at the same time, not to settle for the status quo. There are ways to overcome these problems, and these ways are the substance of this book.

Peter L.'s story can help you anticipate some of the difficulties. Each difficulty can get in the way of your desire to be a resourceful and distinctively Christian caregiver. If you find something of yourself in one or more of these difficulties, forgive yourself for being human, and read on. The Lord isn't merely gritting his teeth and using imperfect humans: he likes it that way! He promises: "My grace is sufficient for you, for my power is made perfect in weakness" (2 Cor. 12:9).

Personal Embarrassment

Being distinctively Christian is sometimes threatening. Our embarrassment is either something we learn as children or part of human nature. In my experience as a psychologist, I have discovered that people often find it easier to talk about sex and sexuality than about faith, religion, or their relationship with God.

Acculturation—learning by observation of role models and social experiences—is no doubt one reason for this. From childhood many have felt awkward, hypersensitive, and embarrassed about spiritual matters. It is easy to understand why these feelings exist if people you respect have shown embarrassment when talking about their faith (or avoided the subject altogether).

Recognizing that many others have a problem with uptightness and self-consciousness, you are better equipped to address these difficulties and begin to overcome them. You will at least have your degree of discomfort reduced, which should help you relax and be easier on yourself.

Others' Embarrassment

The embarrassment of others can be contagious. Having gained confidence in your distinctively Christian contribution, you might come into a situation as a caring person with high aspirations, only to find that you are influenced by the other person's uptightness when anything concerning faith or religion is mentioned. It is like feeding squirrels in the park. The squirrel wants what you have but isn't quite sure you can be trusted. You want the squirrel to take the peanut from your fingers, but if the squirrel makes a sudden move, so do you—and then it takes a long time to reestablish trust between you. The squirrel will be even more tentative, and so will you.

Positive contagion, however, can work just like negative contagion. I have talked with people whose faith was such a natural part of them that I became more comfortable as we discussed matters of religion and spirituality.

Excessive Caution

This difficulty results from the desire not to be overbearing. Like Peter L., many of us don't want to "push our faith down anyone's throat." This is understandable, but the result sometimes can be to err in the opposite direction by neglecting appropriate opportunities to be demonstrably Christian. Caution is sometimes called for, but so is boldness. To guide yourself, you need to be attuned to opportunities for using the Christian resources at your disposal while remaining sensitive to the dignity and needs of each individual to whom you relate.

A Bad Experience

Having a bad experience with someone who is extremely pushy can make you "gun-shy." You are so determined not to be like "them" that you freeze up completely when it comes to relating to others in a distinctively Christian way.

Insufficient Knowledge

Education offered in churches and other religious institutions or in Christian homes does not always satisfy the need for knowledge that will serve you well in caring for others. You can be well-equipped with Bible knowledge (verses memorized, for instance) and still find your knowledge inadequate when you are faced with someone's deep spiritual need. You can know the doctrine of your church and its history, yet still flounder for a response when someone turns to you in pain and turmoil, seeking comfort. I do not intend to demean memorizing Bible verses or learning church history; these efforts can be rewarding and worthwhile. What is often lacking is how to apply Christian resources to the deep and complex needs of people.

There is a positive side to this difficulty: when lack of knowledge is a problem, good education and training can do much. You will need to work at it, but your efforts will yield many benefits.

Fear of Mishandling Explosive Materials

Sometimes we treat Christian resources too gingerly. We try to distance ourselves from distinctively Christian ways of relating, almost regarding these tools and methods as though they were radioactive or highly volatile. You might experience this difficulty, saying to yourself in effect, "I know better than to play with fire."

This is false, even though it shows proper regard for the great power unleashed by Christian resources. One of these resources is *forgiveness,* and it is meant for you. You can make mistakes and be forgiven, time after time. Certainly there are risks involved whenever you relate to others in any way, including sharing your faith. But as a child of God you are called to take those risks, and you are assured in advance of forgiveness.

The decision is similar to the one you had to make when you first learned to drive or were first trusted to use a sharp knife. A car misused can be lethal, and a knife carelessly wielded is dangerous. Nevertheless, most people accept the accompanying risks and responsibilities in order to use these tools for the good they do and the convenience they offer. So it is with the tools of faith. You can learn how to use them responsibly, and when you do, you will be more effective in caring for others, which is what God has called you to do.

You can trust yourself in matters of Christian caring, because God trusts you and is himself trustworthy. God tenderly invites you to trust that he is your loving parent. This means that God chooses to risk letting you be on your own with the power he gives you—with his guidance, under his care, and assured of his love.

Fear of Rejection

Fear of rejection when you relate to others in specifically Christian ways is another difficulty. Most of the time this fear is unwarranted. You are merely being too cautious. Furthermore, you can greatly decrease the probability of a poor reception by listening to others and responding to their needs. People will frequently communicate to you by their actions or their demeanor whether they are comfortable with Christian sharing. If you're not sure about their receptivity, it doesn't hurt to ask.

Pausing to listen to another's needs and responding to them does not mean that you are hiding your light under a bushel. You need to be sensitive in your caring and relating. Beware of the heavy-handed, bull-in-a-china-shop approach in which you are so insensitive to others that you turn them off to Christianity. Be sensitive to the need for appropriate timing; listen. If you do not, you might well experience rejection, because you are trying to fulfill your own needs, not the needs of others.

Mislabeling and Misdefining

You might already be caring in a distinctively Christian way and simply not recognize that you are doing so. Peter L.'s attitude toward his involvement with the mentally retarded children is an example of this. Living out your faith can be done in a number of ways; it does not always have to be couched in prayer, Bible reading, or specific talk about God. A "cup of cold water" at the right time and place can be the mark that sets you apart as a distinctively Christian carer, as Jesus observes in Mark 9:41. Furthermore, your vocation can be distinctively Christian in and of itself. Elton Trueblood said, "Secular work well done is 'holy enterprise'!"

Paralyzing Perfectionism

You prefer that your auto mechanic never makes a mistake. Nevertheless you admit the possibility, given the complexity of the situations with which he or she deals. You know that the mechanic will sometimes be mistaken and can still be an acceptable representative of his or her profession. But a minister, a priest, or you, a Christian caregiver, make mistakes? Never! This demand for perfection can paralyze you into inactivity. The exact opposite is true—your Christianity enables you to take even more risks. You occasionally will make mistakes. But be sure of this: your acceptability to God does not depend on your performance as a Christian caregiver, but on his prior decision to embrace you in his love.

Image Preservation

Sometimes people have difficulty being distinctively Christian because they want to appear cool, suave, sophisticated. Fortunately, the atmosphere has changed somewhat in the last few years. To be thought of as religious nowadays is less likely to invite ridicule or insults than it was a short time ago. If you are concerned about your image sometimes—and who isn't—perhaps you will agree with this observation: the people you admire the most are usually characterized by congruence or genuineness. Who they say they are and what they do match up. My guess is the more you achieve congruence—distinctively Christian congruence—the more respect you will receive.

Then again, sometimes you will not be respected despite your personal integration. At that point you need to ask yourself, "What do I want more—self-respect, or the respect of others?"

Uncertainty of Others' Needs

If you don't know what someone else needs, ask. For example, if you think someone might benefit by your sharing experiences from your own faith-life, you might say:

> As we've been talking, I was wondering if it might be helpful for me to share some of the struggles I had with my faith over the years, and where I am right now. I'm not saying you should think or act exactly as I did, but it could give you some insights into what you might do.

Talking about the difficulties we face as Christian caregivers can lead to pessimism or gloom, but the difficulties need to be out in the open. Just seeing them in the cold light of day can be enough to dispel some. For others, you may need to know more about how to deal with them. After warning you about these problems, I now want to elaborate on what it means to be distinctively Christian.

2

God as the Curegiver

Farmers teach lessons in hope every day. They toil for days, even weeks, preparing the soil for planting. Tilling, fertilizing, planting seeds, using herbicides and insecticides, and culti-vating—all these activities work to prepare, nourish, and pro-tect the crop. And every day, farmers hope—for rain, but not too much, for sun, but not too much, for warmth, but not too much. When the time for harvest arrives, farmers know they are gathering in hopes fulfilled as much as work rewarded.

The apostle Paul knew this. In 1 Cor. 3:6-7 he wrote, "I planted, Apollos watered, but God gave the growth. So neither he who plants nor he who waters is anything, but only God who gives the growth." As a farmer's responsibility rests with preparing a crop for harvest, so the Christian caregiver's re-sponsibility is to "plant" and "water." God then provides the growth. In other words, *Christians are responsible for care; God is responsible for cure*.

What Christian caregivers do is prepare the ground for the Great Curegiver. Preparing the ground means doing the best possible job to create a therapeutic situation and then waiting on the Lord expectantly. It is God who provides emotional, mental, physical, and spiritual growth according to his will.

The word therapy is derived from the Greek word *therapeuo,* which means "to serve," "to restore," "to care for," "to wait upon," or "to treat medically." Whether you are clergy or lay, pro or semipro, you are a Christian therapist. This role, which may be new to you, is your response to the presence of Jesus Christ in your life: a response of service to others.

Therapeuo is a relationship word. A therapist, therefore, is a person whose relationships with others are characterized by service and caring. That's a pretty good working definition of a Christian; therefore, you are a therapist. In common usage, the Greek word *therapeuo* connotes "willingness to serve." In this sense anyone involved in the process of caring for another is involved in doing therapy.

Along with being a relationship or process word, *therapeuo* is also a result word. For the Greeks, medical treatment (therapy) was associated with results, with providing a cure. This is also the emphasis in the New Testament use of the word *therapeuo.* It speaks of cures and healing provided by Jesus Christ. Results did not come through the abilities or wisdom of people (not even the 12 disciples), but from God.

Understanding what therapy is from a biblical perspective will help you see what makes Christian care distinctive. Like other caregivers, Christians work hard to establish relationships that build up people in need. Christian caregivers, however, rely on God for results.

In the broadest sense, what you are offering in distinctively Christian caring is love. Because Jesus Christ lives in you, you are God's ambassador. You carry the news of his unconditional acceptance and hope-filled gospel of forgiveness and life in him. Caring is a process—like tilling, fertilizing, planting, and cultivating. Processes are verbs, and the process of caring is in your hands. Results are nouns, and cures (the results of your caring) are in God's hands.

Living out the knowledge that results—cures—belong to God is living in faith. Such faith has beneficial effects on both the caregiver and the person receiving care.

For the Caregiver

When you as caregiver realize that God is the Curegiver, you are freed from worry and false expectations. Demands on yourself to get results are silenced, and so are any demands for the care receiver to shape up or change. Instead, you can concentrate on creating the best therapeutic situation for growth to occur: developing trust and communicating acceptance and love.

If you do not rely on God to provide the results, you are in for trouble. There are only two other places to look for success. First, you can become self-oriented and pressured from within, trying to force people to grow or change through your help. Weighted down by this responsibility, you fall into worry about results or increasing self-doubts about your ability as a caregiver. This cycle of doubt and worry can lead you to become increasingly self-absorbed and consequently less caring.

Second, you can place responsibility for success on the one receiving care. If you choose this course, what first seems like a great relief—at least it is no longer up to you—will eventually leave you frustrated and exasperated. God has provided human beings with many inner resources to cope and change. Yet people broken by sin and problems in life will not be able to pull themselves up by their own bootstraps, nor should you expect them to do so. The healing power of God is needed.

Trusting God to provide results means freedom for you, the caregiver. Yet freedom is not license. Ceasing to worry about results does not entitle you to provide careless care. Although God provides the growth, being a good farmer is hard work.

So is being a good carer. Good preachers surely trust in the Holy Spirit to use their words, yet they still go into the pulpit well prepared. Your motivation and preparation is not diminished when you rely on God as the curegiver; rather, your reliance on God empowers your preparation.

For the Care Receiver

Understanding that God is the Curegiver also benefits the person receiving care. Reliance on God provides tremendous freedom to grow and change through a helping relationship. The person receiving care does not have to push too hard for growth and change. Rather, the person is free to receive God's love through the caregiver. The person receiving care will be able to risk change, realizing that God will provide the cure.

The care receiver has plenty of responsibilities without the added burden of total accountability for results. First, the one receiving care already has a problem that causes the need for care. Second, receiving love from a caregiver is easier said than done. When we need to receive love, we may seem to be weak and vulnerable. People don't like being in that position, so being open to receiving care is a formidable task.

The care receiver is subject to the same temptations to shift blame as the caregiver. The care receiver could expect the caregiver to be a miracle worker who will provide all the results. When results don't come rapidly enough, the person could become angry with the caregiver and thereby disrupt the helping process.

Freedom from responsibility for results does not provide an escape for the care receiver either. Being a recipient of care does not mean the person is simply acted upon. The one receiving care still needs to work hard at expressing feelings, sharing self, being honest, and being open to receiving care.

The freedom provided by trust in the almighty Curegiver is not freedom to be irresponsible. God is providing the freedom to participate in and receive care. It is freedom that commits the whole person to the healing process.

In Chapter 18, ''Celebrating Results,'' you will learn about what can happen when you care in a distinctively Christian way. For now, what you need to know is whose results those are. They are the Lord's—the same Lord who is your Shepherd, who walks with you through the valley of the shadow of death. Realizing that God is the Curegiver, you are freer to accept the responsibility to care. With this knowledge, you will find that the yoke laid on you is easier to bear.

3

God, You, and Me

There is a psychotherapy technique called cotherapy, in which two therapists work simultaneously with a client. Although it is used infrequently, the cotherapy approach has a number of advantages. Two sets of listening ears are less likely to miss something significant said by the client. Also, two psychotherapists can sometimes better help the client in necessary problem solving. Moreover, when two therapists with different personal and theoretical perspectives counsel with a client, they bring complementary insights to the caring situation.

Although cotherapy has only recently been recognized and used in psychotherapy, it nonetheless is no new discovery. The practice has been around quite a while in the Judeo-Christian tradition: "in an abundance of counselors there is safety" (Prov. 11:14).

As a Christian caregiver, you are never alone. God is always present with you as cotherapist, as cocaregiver. God is always there—whether you realize it or not, whether you acknowledge him or not. When you identify and integrate God's presence in your caring and relating, the impact of his presence on you and your caring relationships can be an empowering force.

24

How Is God Present?

God, who is present everywhere without being any more present in one place than another, still shows himself to be present in special ways at various times. Here are three ways you can experience this special, paradoxical presence of God in the caring process.

Like a Senior Surgeon

God's presence can be felt like that of a senior surgeon supervising resident physicians in training. Before surgical residents enter the operating room, the senior surgeon has already given them careful instruction and guidance. When the residents are called on to perform an operation, the senior surgeon is frequently there—overseeing, giving instructions where necessary, and providing them with the security that comes from knowing someone is present with expertise they do not yet possess. Should a situation occur that a surgical resident is unequipped to handle, the senior surgeon can carefully and skillfully guide the resident's hand, talking him or her through the procedure. If necessary, the senior surgeon can take over.

One might even go so far as to say that the wisdom of the senior surgeon finds expression in the resident's fingers. Likewise, the presence and wisdom of God expresses itself through you as you relate to and care for others. It is certainly your hands that do the work, but without God's wisdom and guidance in and with you, you would be very much alone. With it, you possess a powerful and distinctively Christian resource.

Like a Wounded Healer

God is also present like a "wounded healer," to use Henri Nouwen's term. The image of a senior surgeon might suggest a superhero who struts around, never touched by the cares and concerns of this world, providing expertise from an unlimited data bank of knowledge and skills.

Most certainly, God is omniscient and omnipotent, but he is hardly distant. He is also present as a wounded healer, who in Jesus Christ shared the problems of life. Not only did he share them but he took them on himself.

> But he was wounded for our transgressions, he was bruised for our iniquities; upon him was the chastisement that made us whole, and with his stripes we are healed (Isa. 53:5).

Here we encounter the wondrous paradox that God is not merely a senior surgeon with infinite wisdom and confident presence; he is also the patient. Jesus himself speaks of this:

> For I was hungry and you gave me food, I was thirsty and you gave me drink, I was a stranger and you welcomed me, I was naked and you clothed me, I was sick and you visited me, I was in prison and you came to me (Matt. 25:35-36).

The people respond to this great compliment with: "Lord, when . . . ?"

His answer: "Truly, I say to you, as you did it to one of the least of these my brethren, you did it to me."

Jesus Christ is present in you as you care for others and in those for whom you care. This is another way he manifests his comforting presence. He has been there himself. He knows what suffering is all about.

Like an Art Nouveau Chair

An *art nouveau* chair I once saw symbolizes another way God is present in caring relationships. The chair was soft and comfortable and had the outline of a hand painted on it. It seemed to invite everyone to relax in its palm. God's presence is like that. Jesus promised, "No one shall snatch them out of my hand" (John 10:28). He provides all the warmth and comfort of your favorite chair as he reminds you that he holds you, the care receiver, the situation, and the whole world in his hands: "The eternal God is your dwelling place, and underneath are the everlasting arms" (Deut. 33:27). As you and the care receiver each nestle in the comfort of God's presence, you experience his wholeness filling your being. An old Irish blessing expresses this:

> May the road rise up to meet you, may the wind be always at your back, the sunshine warm upon your face, the rainfall soft upon your field. And until we meet again, may God hold you in the palm of his hand.

Practicalizing God's Presence

Here are some ways that you can draw from God's presence and put his presence into action.

Through Prayer

One way of coming alive to the presence of God in a caring relationship is through prayer. Many people who do not experience God's presence in their lives express the feeling of being lost in the universe. Those who lack purpose and meaning feel the "lostness" that William Adam Brown described in *The Life of Prayer in a World of Science:*

> In the last analysis, it comes to this: either we are alone in the universe, facing its unsolved mysteries and its appalling tragedies with only the help that comes from other mortals as ignorant and as helpless as we, or there is

Someone who hears us when we speak and answers when we call.

Brown concluded:

The man who has learned to pray is no longer alone in the universe. He is living in his father's house.

Prayer can be a primary means for realizing that both you and the care receiver live, move, and have your being in your "Father's house."

Through a Heightened Consciousness of God's Presence

Brother Lawrence, a 17th-century monk, worked in the kitchen of a monastery in southern France. In the midst of the simplest, most routine tasks he learned to "practice the presence of God."

God is present in your life and caring relationships, whether you take note of him or not, but a heightened consciousness of God's presence can cultivate in you, the caregiver, and in the care receiver as well, an attitude of trust in God.

By Verbalizing God's Presence

Another important aspect of coming alive to God's presence is actually mentioning the fact of his presence. If you ever walked through an art museum, you were probably awed by the beautiful, priceless works of art you viewed. If you had the opportunity to tour the museum again with a well-informed tour guide, the same works of art probably became more meaningful for you. The same is true in a helping relationship. God is certainly there and can be experienced even when he is not specifically identified or discussed. When his presence in that caring relationship is appropriately identified, however, it can become all the more significant. Such verbalizing can open up new perspectives and avenues of caring.

This truth was powerfully brought home to me recently by Ann, one of my clients. Just as I was putting the finishing touches on this chapter, Ann was in the process of terminating several years of psychotherapy with me. As we went about concluding our therapy and going through the process of saying good-bye, a serious crisis occurred in Ann's life. I was concerned that this crisis would affect her adversely, perhaps throwing her into an emotional tailspin. Quite the contrary. Although she certainly did experience sadness, anxiety, and frustration with the situation (a perfectly natural response to the situation), she was able to handle the crisis extremely well.

I felt pleased that the five years of therapy seemed to have worked and that her growth was not just temporary. I remember saying, "It looks as if we have done our work well."

Ann smiled and said:

I think it was really God who did it. There were times when I felt so low, so despondent, so out of control that I didn't know what to do. I have an idea that at those times you didn't know what to do with me either. I really believe that God was with me when neither I nor you knew what to do—that God was the one providing the therapy during those times. I think we both have done a good job. You have been a good therapist to me and I have worked very hard myself. I've taken a lot of risks and shared with you a lot of scary and personal things about myself. But we need to give credit where credit is due, and that is with God.

What a tremendous profession of faith that was! Ann testified that God was present—helping, guiding, and comforting both me as caregiver and her as care receiver throughout the caring relationship. And so it is with you.

4

Why Care?

Professional caregivers often press clients to delve into their motivations—to explore in depth what beliefs, attitudes, or philosophy of life cause them to act in a certain way. When they are similarly pressed to consider their own motivations, the results can be enlightening. Consider my experience with a young man I'll call Jim.

Jim was a university student. He came to me for therapy at the suggestion of a counselor at the university. Although most of the people I see in my part-time practice as a clinical psychologist are Christians, Jim was not. He was a Jew.

When Jim came to me, he was anxious and at times depressed. This was interfering with his studies and his sleep. It was also causing him to be irritable with his roommate and other friends.

At first Jim complained that others were placing unrealistic demands on him. Later we discovered together that he was the one making the unrealistic demands. Jim was a perfectionist. When he did not meet his own standards of perfection, anxiety and depression would set in. In time through this discovery and others which he gained from therapy, Jim was able to study better, sleep more, get along better with his peers, and generally feel more at ease with himself.

As our therapy relationship continued, Jim developed a high degree of trust in me. About this time he began talking about some of his spiritual concerns and what his religious heritage meant to him. He shared with me a paper he had written on the subject in high school. It was obvious that this was not simply an objective research paper but an expression of his own deep feelings.

Jim's sharing his spiritual concerns did not surprise me. People in therapy frequently begin by dealing with more or less purely psychological or psychiatric issues, but eventually move into the realm of the religious or spiritual. This echoes the observation made by Carl Jung in *Modern Man in Search of a Soul*:

> Among all the patients in the second half of life—that is to say, over 35—there has not been one whose problem in the last resort was not that of finding a religious outlook on life. It is safe to say that every one of them fell ill because he had lost that which the living religions of every age have given to their followers. And none of them has been really healed who did not regain his religious outlook.

Discussions of spiritual and faith issues have always been exciting and stimulating for me as a therapist and as a minister. Sharing in Jim's spiritual search was particularly rewarding for me, as it ultimately touched on my own spirituality.

We had been discussing spiritual issues on and off for some time, when at the beginning of one of our therapy sessions, Jim asked me, "Why are you a psychologist?"

I felt pleased that Jim had asked that question. I told him I became a psychologist because I was interested in people and desired to be involved in helping others deal with their life struggles and problems.

"I understand that," Jim said, "But why are you a psychologist?"

"Well, I very much enjoy working with people," I said. "It gives me a great deal of satisfaction to think that I might have played a significant part in helping others to have a more fulfilling life."

"Yes, but why are you a psychologist?" Jim persisted. "Why do you do what you do?"

I realized that Jim wanted to hear about something other than the academic, professional, or even altruistic interests that led me to be a psychologist. I had an idea he wanted to know why I, a *person*, was involved in the whole of the psychotherapy process—what deep personal satisfaction I derived from my work.

I thought for a few seconds and replied, "Being a psychologist gives me the opportunity to deal with situations and people not just from a distance or on a surface level, but to get involved with them in a real and personal way. For me, being a psychologist means not only doing something to or even for another person, but being involved with someone as a fellow human being. I am a psychologist not only because I enjoy the academic discipline and am interested in the professional techniques, but especially because of who I am to another person in the process."

I sat back rather pleased with my answer. I thought I had given Jim a dynamic and power-packed answer about who I am—both as a person and psychologist.

But Jim still was not satisfied. "Yes, I think I understand what you are saying," he said. "We've touched on some of those things before, and I respect and appreciate you not only for your professional expertise, but also for who you are. But,

I still want to know what it is that really motivates you. What primary force lies behind your life and work? Why do you do what you do?''

I began to sense that Jim's question was even more deeply probing than I first thought. Remembering some of our previous conversations about his own spiritual and religious concerns, I realized that he was asking me about my ultimates— about those things that motivate me from very deep down— or very high up.

As I thought again about Jim's question, I realized that I indeed had an answer. It was meaningful for me, but undoubtedly would not have the same inner meaning for him. I asked myself whether I should go ahead and give him that answer. On the one hand, I did not want to offend him. On the other, I wanted to relate to him as honestly as I wanted him to relate to me.

"Jim," I said, "I think I see what you are asking now. I hope you know me well enough by now to know that I am not the kind of person who would try to bully you with my personal feelings about my faith. But in order to answer your question, I need to share with you some of my deeper convictions. Then, if you like, we can talk about it. The reason I am a psychologist lies in my faith in God and in what God has done for me in Jesus Christ. I believe that Jesus cares for me so much that he was willing to give his life for me. Remembering his love, I can't help but reach out and share that love and care with others. So that is why I do what I do. That is why I am a psychologist.''

"OK," Jim responded. "I just wanted to know.''

That was the extent of his response, and I was surprised that he did not pursue the matter further. I suppose I expected him to be somewhat taken aback by my answer, and I was also slightly fearful that he might be offended by what I said. In a later session, however, he told me that he had asked that question because he was genuinely interested in who I was as a spiritual human being. He also said that he respected me for my religious convictions, even though they were not the same as his.

The Distinctiveness of Christian Care

Anyone involved in caring needs to ask "Why do I do what I do?" For Christians, the answer to this question is quite a distinctive one. About 2000 years ago, God identified himself fully with our humanness. He sent his Son into the world to live and breathe, to suffer and love, to minister and care—and finally to die. Jesus' death appeared to be just another human tragedy. But death could not hold down the one who is Life. Rising triumphantly from the grave, Jesus established his church.

Through his church Jesus continues to extend his ministry of love and care for people. The love of Christ is powerful and dynamic. It is not just a good feeling; it is the basic motivation for all Christian caring. This is summarized in 1 John 4:19: "We love because he first loved us."

The distinctiveness of Christian care, then, lies not only in what we do, but in why we do it. As the message of God's love grips Christians, we are filled by the Holy Spirit, who moves clay-footed Christians to use our God-given gifts for others. He makes cared-for Christians into caring Christians.

Think back for a moment to the answers I gave to Jim's questions. Only the last answer set me apart as a distinctively Christian caregiver, because that answer finally revealed my ultimate motivation to Jim.

Benefits of a Solid Foundation

It is profoundly important that you, a distinctively Christian caregiver, recognize the basic motivation for why you do what you do. It can profoundly influence your attitudes and actions. When you realize that Jesus' love is the foundation of what you do, then:

● You have a clearer sense of identity as a caregiver. You realize that you are an extension of Christ's ministry, under his leadership and empowered by his love.

● You are provided with an attitude of humility and servanthood. You find yourself reaching out to others not with a sense of superiority, but with a desire to serve.

● You gain assurance of strength and power. Caring in many situations is fraught with frustrations and difficulties. If you rely solely on your own resources, you can become weary or give up. Yet you always have Christ in you providing his love—which never quits when the going gets rough.

● You receive a new perspective on caring. Acts of love and caring often do not show visible results. It is tempting to say, ''What's the use?'' When you realize that your caring is motivated and empowered by Jesus Christ, you know that he is the one who provides the results. He is working in every situation. And you are thus uplifted by Christ's love to continue your acts of caring.

While it is important for you to see clearly your basic Christian motivation, it is not always necessary to share this with the person for whom you are caring. You must gain the right to share your faith with another—by your perception of the other's needs, by the depth of your relationship with the other, or by the other person asking you.

Sharing Your Motivation

To help you determine when it would be appropriate, necessary, and desirable to share the ultimate reason for your caring, I offer these basic guidelines:

● *Evaluate the other person's needs.* Make sure when you share your basic motivation, it is what the other person needs to hear, not simply what you want them to hear.

● *Consider the relationship.* Perhaps the relationship has reached such depth that it is natural for you to share your spiritual motivations. Your relationship might have reached the point where you are impelled to share your faith in Jesus Christ to go further.

● *Answer questions when you are asked.* When someone asks a question of you, as Jim did of me, then an open door is provided for your sharing.

Your ultimate motivation for caring is Jesus Christ. He provides purpose and power so that your caring relationships are transformed by his love. Knowing this will affect your identity, attitude, confidence, and perspective as a caregiver.

5

Family Ties

While in graduate school, I taught an introductory college psychology course at a community center. All my students were black. In fact, almost everyone connected with the community center was black. From the time I arrived at the center until I returned home, I rarely saw another white person.

Going to my classroom one evening, I saw a security guard coming up the stairs toward me. He was white. My immediate response was a friendly "Hello!" He responded in kind. After we passed, I wondered about my enthusiastic greeting. The reason for it—and probably his as well—was that we were both Caucasian, surrounded by many people who were not.

Such behavior based on color indicates that there is a certain commonality or "community" transcending any previous contact or lack of it. There is a certain shared experience in being white, as there is a certain shared experience in being black.

You probably have noticed the same dynamics among alumni of educational institutions, members of fraternities, or other special-interest groups. Whenever they meet, they feel an immediate bond. Alumni or fraternity members don't need to have been students together. Their bond transcends time and geography.

Human longings to identify with a group also are evident in the perpetuation of the various Christian denominations. Although some aspects of denominationalism are unhealthy, other aspects are good. For example, the traditions represented by different denominations allow Christians to identify with a variety of worship styles, musical heritages, and social concerns.

On a broader and higher level, I believe that the same dynamics operate in all of us as Christians. Those of us who accept Jesus Christ as our personal Savior can be considered members of the same family.

We Are All Members of the Body of Christ

The Scriptures describe the Christian family in a variety of ways. One of the most powerful metaphors for this is used by the apostle Paul, who states that every Christian is a part of the body of Christ (1 Cor. 12:27). Just as the human body has many parts, so it is with the body of Christ (12:12). It encompasses people of vastly different ethnic groups, cultures, ages, abilities, and interests. Yet this heterogeneous body is a unity (12:13). Jesus has connected every believer with himself in such an intimate way that he lives in us and we in him. In a burst of creative love God has suddenly laced us fragmented, lonely humans to himself and to each other with threads of gold.

The bonds of the whole Christian family fashioned by the power and love of Jesus Christ are distinct from those of other groups. All Christians are involved in a unique web of relationships that transcend the normal barriers of human prejudice.

A recent experience demonstrated some of the richness in being with strangers who are fellow Christians. I had occasion to consult in another city with an urban congregation that was developing a community counseling center. Part of my task was to arrive early to get the feel of their overall ministry by participating in some of their activities.

I flew into town on the afternoon of Ash Wednesday. I remember feeling sad because I could not be with my family in our own congregation for the fellowship meal and evening service. Yet I also felt a certain warmth and security in knowing that I would be with a Christian congregation.

As it turned out, I attended the other congregation's evening meal and worship and felt very much a part of it. When we concluded the consultation the next day, I thanked them for their hospitality and shared how I considered that their congregation was actually mine for that 24-hour period. It was like a "home away from home." When I went forward to receive a blessing and a cross of ashes on my forehead, as is the custom in my own tradition, I knew that at about the same time my family was doing the same at our own church. I was really not worshiping apart from my family that evening, but together with them and with the Christian church all over the world. Transcending time zones and borders, cultural or racial differences, Christians were worshiping as one body that evening.

Caring Relationships within the Body of Christ

The term *body of Christ* describes people united by Jesus Christ into a real community. This "family-ness" of Christianity entails both benefits and responsibilities. We are called to move beyond mere superficial relationships with others to discover what in-depth caring is all about.

We caring Christians follow the example of our Lord Jesus. He loved. He grieved. He became angry. He nurtured. All of these are elements of deep relationships. Jesus did not mince words, but went straight to the heart—getting people to think about themselves, their faith, and their relationship to him and his kingdom.

The idea of family has many implications for us as we go about caring for and relating to others. The distinctive reality of the Christian community can positively affect both the caregiver and the one receiving care.

A Right and Responsibility to Care

Even Christian caregivers sometimes find themselves asking questions like "What right do I have to involve myself in another person's life?" or "What right do I have to pry into another person's affairs?" The question is really: "What right do I have to care for another person?"

Ultimately, the right to care flows from our responsibility as family members. It is God who created the Christian family. He desires you and me to reach into the lives of our fellow family members with his love. In a certain way, we have a "license to care" closely connected with the bonds of community that God establishes among Christians.

We have the responsibility to care based on the needs of people. Frequently I find that people, especially those who are hurting, want to talk about their needs. Although they may flinch when you first ask about what deeply concerns them most, they will later express relief and be grateful that you cared enough to ask, listen, and help them to deal with their concerns. Widows and widowers frequently complain that after their spouse's death, friends and other concerned people seem reluctant to talk about the deceased. Contrary to what you might think, most widowed people want to talk about the significant other they have lost.

In general, people desire the loving care of fellow Christians. It is our privilege and responsibility to share this.

A Head Start of Trust and Rapport

Care from a fellow Christian is like care from a member of your family. Because the caregiver and the care receiver are members of the same family, trust is established from the start. The helping relationship does not start from scratch. A degree of rapport is already present through common faith in Jesus Christ.

At times it might be beneficial for you, the caregiver, to verbalize that you and the one receiving care are members of the same family, the body of Christ. I believe that this can do much to put the care receiver at ease from the start, maybe you as well.

Caring for Another Member of the Christian Family

An important principle of psychotherapy or counseling is that it is not good for a counselor to do therapy with a member of his or her immediate family, a relative, close friend, or associate. This is a good practice to follow. Therapy with someone close to you can be less effective. It can also be dangerous. For healthy objectivity to exist, the therapist must not be too emotionally involved with the client.

From another point of view it is unfortunate that most professional therapists do not have any prior relationship with their clients. It generally takes a while for clients to learn to trust their therapist enough to discuss their personal problems deeply and begin to grow.

Those who acknowledge they are members of the Christian family and enter into a caring relationship enjoy both advantages. They experience some closeness or commonality through their Christian family membership, but the caregiver still enters the relationship with a healthy emotional distance.

In this sense Christian caregivers frequently are able to combine the better from both worlds, drawing on the advantages of mutual membership in the Christian family and an objectivity that permits a healthy, therapeutic relationship.

Christ created a community in our midst; he wants us to appreciate what this means. We act on our sense of community when we build deep, loving relationships with other Christians. In a family with a loving Father, a giving Brother, and an empowering Spirit, can we do otherwise?

6

Move Over, Freud!

Sometimes I think of sending this letter to Sigmund Freud, the founder of the modern mental health movement:

Dear Sigmund,

I admit that the techniques and insights you and your followers have developed are vital to the treatment of troubled people. But there are questions of life, death, meaning, and spirituality that you never touch.

Sincerely,
Ken

Disciples of Sigmund Freud often claim that the only real, nonsuperficial way to diagnose and treat the individual is to employ psychoanalytic perspectives and techniques: that is, investigating the unconscious, focusing on childhood, dream analysis, and free association. "We know where the action is," they seem to say. "It's infantile sexuality, libido, the Oedipus complex, and ego defense mechanisms. If you are unwilling to tackle the problem at those depths, you're just playing around."

While the Freudian system does have value, and in many ways is indeed a deep system, when compared to the uniquely Christian system of caring for the individual, it is quite superficial. Infantile sexuality and libido do not seem so deep next to the basic questions and concerns of life, death, spirituality, and meaning. These latter issues reach down to the deepest level of our beings—beyond the unconscious.

Before continuing, I want to make it clear that I do not refer to the Freudian psychoanalytic system alone. The same applies to a number of psychological systems: Rogerian, Behavioral, Gestalt, Rational-Emotive, Transactional Analysis, and Neo-Analytic to name a few. I believe each of these systems has a unique and valuable contribution to make. Nevertheless, these approaches appear quite superficial when compared to the unique Christian perspective.

That is, no doubt, my Christian bias. I remind you, however, that I share this bias with you not only as a fellow Christian and ordained minister, but as a secularly trained psychologist.

The Advantages of Christian Caregiving

My point is this: all other factors being equal, Christian caregiving has significant advantages over any other method. The primary advantage is that of depth. I do not make this assertion lightly; it is the primary thesis of this book. Christian caregiving is superior to caregiving of any other kind.

There are two ways to view what I am saying. You could say: "What a brash and narrow-minded claim!" On the other hand, you might say: "I would certainly expect that the author of *Christian Caregiving—a Way of Life* believes this. I wonder why he is making such an issue over something so obvious."

Here is why. All too often, Christian caregivers consider the impact of their caring to be comparatively insignificant. They believe that they are inadequate because they are not as well versed in psychological theories as secular professionals. Specifically, they think that without extensive secular education, they cannot relate deeply to those for whom they care.

Not so at all! Christian caregivers need to feel good about their unique orientation. They need to realize that the distinctively Christian approach is the deepest system available. Of course, the techniques and perspective of psychology can be helpful. However, the best content and framework on which to build is the Christian one. I also believe that psychology needs theology to realize its greatest potential. In my experience, the best secular psychotherapists are those who are conversant in religious and theological matters.

Christians need to feel good about themselves and the caring they give. There is simply no reason for a person who is able to provide distinctively Christian care to be self-demeaning.

Of course, there is the other side of the coin. Christian caregivers who have failed to do their homework—that is, who do not understand their own unique identity—have every right to feel ashamed. To be truly effective, you need to be clear about your identity as a distinctively Christian caregiver and actively live out that unique orientation.

Being and acting in a distinctively Christian manner is not easy. It requires study. Perhaps one reason why secular caregivers *seem to be* more competent in their areas is because they truly *are*. Christian caregivers—whether nonprofessional, semiprofessional, or professional—must be well-versed in their own area of expertise. Otherwise, the potential may be there, but it will never be realized.

The intrinsic beauty of Christian caring might be likened to a diamond. The intrinsic beauty of caring offered by others might be compared to a sapphire. Neither stone in its natural state is properly cut and polished. Both need work. Which is more valuable—a diamond or a sapphire? Most people would say, "A diamond." But if the diamond was unpolished and the sapphire was polished, the sapphire probably would be preferred. It takes "polishing" for a distinctively Christian caregiver to display his or her beauty.

Recovering Our Heritage

Christians need to recover something that they once possessed, but recently lost: theology as the primary source out of which caring and counseling flows. From the New Testament era to the recent past, Christian caregiving drew on theology as the primary basis for the content of caring and counseling. In the last 50 to 75 years, however, emphasis has shifted from a theological to a psychological basis for "Christian" caring and counseling.

Again, I wish to emphasize that there is nothing wrong with using psychological insights—even rather extensively. Psychology has contributed significantly both to the development of humanity in general and to the development of caring and counseling in the church. But I think we have thrown out the baby with the bath water. To return to the earlier analogy, we have acquired a sapphire, but lost a diamond—our own diamond. We have come to think that we can understand and care for people without touching their spiritual, ethical, or theological dimensions.

To be sure, Christians have their faults—legalism and judgmental attitudes, to name but two. Sometimes Christians have been inaccurate in their understanding of a person or situation. But perhaps we Christians have become excessively apologetic and cautious because we recognize that errors have been made. During the same 2000 years of New Testament times, practitioners of other disciplines—for instance, medicine—have made some glaring mistakes: misdiagnoses, treatments that did not help, treatments that actually did more harm than good—sometimes even resulting in the death of the patient.

In his book *The Minister as Diagnostician* Paul Pruyser notes that church people often avoid theology, but he maintains its usefulness. He stresses that Christian caregivers should not depend solely on the terminology of other disciplines and suggests that they can beneficially return to their own, including *grace, repentance, Christian vocation,* and *love.*

As you live a life of distinctively Christian caring, you might occasionally run into situations in which you feel as if you are in over your head. The problems of the person you are caring for may be more than you can handle alone. The individual may need the services of another caregiver—a psychologist, psychiatrist, pastoral counselor, psychiatric social worker, psychiatric nurse, or other similarly-trained professional. Find the best resource for the person in your community and make the referral.

When the care receiver's problems are too deep or complex for you to handle on your own, make the referral without feeling guilty or worrying that your faith is inadequate. There is no need to doubt your calling or ability as a distinctively Christian caregiver. The professional caregiver might offer acquired skills which you might not have, and you offer distinctively Christian caring and resources which many professional caregivers don't have.

Remember also that the person may still need your love, support, and distinctively Christian caregiving. The individual needs as much love and support as before—maybe more. Furthermore, he or she still has spiritual needs which can only be filled by a faith relationship with Jesus Christ as Lord and Savior, and your distinctively Christian caring enables God to speak directly and lovingly to that need—always being careful not to compete or conflict with the work of the other caregiver.

I expect that in years to come theology will play an increasingly greater role, enabling us to understand better the nature of human deficiencies, problems, potentials, and joys. I believe this will affect not only Christians but also those outside the body of Christ.

Psychology, sociology, and medicine cannot give the entire answer to the human condition. There is a significant gap left for theology, and it behooves Christians, both clergy and lay, not to disavow their authority, but to step in and fill that gap.

7

Touching Spiritual Depths

People are units—integrated human beings who have physical, emotional, mental, social, and spiritual needs. "Of course," you say. "How else could it be? Why state the obvious?" Yet, when people stand in need of care, they often find their needs divided among specialists in caregiving. Physicians seize the physical; psychotherapists or counselors, the mental and emotional; friends and family, the social. Perhaps the spiritual goes begging for want of a willing caregiver—or it falls squarely on the shoulders of pastors, whose job descriptions supposedly read, "Spiritual Care Provider."

Every Christian's job description includes being a spiritual care provider. By virtue of your Christian faith, you are uniquely equipped to relate to the deep spiritual needs of others. Your "specialist" function as a Christian caring person can ensure that another's spiritual needs will not be unrecognized and unmet. You are an agent who rightly integrates spiritual needs into the other kinds of care a person might receive.

Before we discuss ways to minister to spiritual needs as one part of the whole person, we need a clearer understanding of what spiritual needs are.

Created by God, people necessarily live their lives in relationship to God. Relationships with God vary significantly among individuals and across time. Some individuals are angry with God and alienated from him, at least part of the time. Others have a relationship that can most kindly be characterized as cool or distant. Still others experience a close relationship with God—finding meaning, purpose, value, and dignity in that relationship. Yet even these people, bonded to God like a child to a parent, find themselves gripped by questions that go to the very heart of their existence:

- What is the meaning of life?
- Why am I here?
- How does God view me?
- What is right, and what is wrong?
- Why does God allow suffering?
- Why must I die?

Some people hope to outgrow these questions—or even claim to have done so. Others try to eliminate their troublesome potential by labeling such questions as sophomoric. But, in fact, these questions affect everyone, and they point to genuine spiritual needs. They cannot be outgrown or put away. They are part of the flow of human life.

In order to understand better what spiritual needs are and how they fit into the human situation, consider this example:

Mr. Adams is hospitalized for a serious illness. It is night-time and his family has gone home. He is alone, lying in bed in the dark, brooding over several pressing concerns. Because his health is threatened, Mr. Adams is concerned about his physical well-being. Because he is alone and separated from his family and friends, he has social needs. Because he can't work, Mr. Adams worries about how to support his family and pay medical bills. Because he is afraid that there is no cure for him, he has many emotional needs.

Lying on his back burdened by all these worries, Mr. Adams is weighed down by a knot of pressing spiritual needs as well. The conflicts and tensions of hospitalization are related to the conflicts and tensions of his relationship with God. Mr. Adams is angry with God because he allowed this to happen. Mr. Adams feels guilty before God because of his angry feelings. He struggles with doubts about his faith. He struggles with the uncertainties of the future, uncertainties that could even include his death.

Mr. Adams needs distinctively Christian caring. Physicians will probe him and prescribe for him; family and friends may sound him out about his mental and emotional state and provide him with companionship. These are all good ways to care. But probably no one will ask him about his standing with God, and the knot of his spiritual needs will remain tied.

Of course, it need not be this way. But too often caregivers neglect ministering to spiritual needs. In fact, even Christian helpers often neglect this aspect of ministry. As a Christian caregiver, you continually need to have your eyes open to the spiritual dimension of people's concerns, along with other dimensions. Even with this knowledge, obstacles to your reaching out to someone's spiritual needs could remain.

Obstacles to Ministering to Spiritual Needs

Although you intellectually see the importance of recognizing and relating to the spiritual needs of people, there are some common roadblocks preventing meaningful spiritual discussion.

Society's Spiritual Impoverishment

One hindrance to freely talking about spiritual needs (for both caregivers and receivers) is that society in general is spiritually impoverished. Spiritual talk, unfortunately, takes a back seat along with distant priorities like "What artists shall the Museum of Modern Art feature in the year 2050?" and "How many metaphysicians can dance on the head of a pensioner?"

Baseball scores, TV shows, stock market performance, recent purchases, behavior of children, and a host of other topics seem more important. People are frequently more comfortable talking about material things than spiritual issues.

Compartmentalization

Related to society's general spiritual impoverishment is a second obstacle: spiritual matters are generally thought to have a place (church) and a time (Sunday). The rest of the world and the rest of the week are reserved for the secular. Splitting apart the spiritual and the secular is unfortunate. Sunday is experienced apart from the reality of the rest of life; Monday through Saturday existence is cut off from the spiritual dimension. Since everyone lives in relationship to God, the spiritual dimension is as much a part of life as any other dimension, regardless of time or place.

Reluctance or Fear

A third obstacle preventing people from addressing spiritual needs is reluctance or fear—on the part of either the caregiver or the care receiver. Discussing personal spiritual needs with someone else can be threatening, because it includes talk about personal and sensitive issues that might not be accepted by others, and it means wrestling with difficult questions affecting the very heart of existence. Frequently, people respond to difficult questions with superficial, pat answers. Stock answers are evidence of the difficulty that many people have in meaningfully discussing spiritual matters. Falling back on canned answers prevents people from examining how they feel inside about their relationship with God, what they really believe.

Lack of Knowledge or Education

Many people do not know, or don't think they know, what to say or do when confronted with others who have spiritual needs. Some people, in fact, are unclear about what spiritual needs are.

Opening the Door for Spiritual Talk

Precisely because society is spiritually impoverished, you, a Christian caring person, need to be ready to open the door for the expression of spiritual needs. The needs are there and must be met. Here are some ways you could begin to initiate spiritual communication.

Provide an Atmosphere of Acceptance

Habits die hard. Because people are in the habit of suppressing their spiritual needs and because society in many ways encourages this, you need to help break this habit. It is important that people know it is acceptable for them to express themselves regarding their spiritual life. In a caring relationship they need to feel an atmosphere of acceptance that explicitly includes talk about their spiritual concerns.

Communicating acceptance, first of all, means taking the time to listen fully, being especially attentive to peoples' hurts and struggles. You might be one of the few who are willing to discuss real spiritual concerns with them. As trust develops, people often become more willing to discuss personal spiritual matters. Your genuineness and willingness to use traditional resources including prayer and the Bible will also help to create an atmosphere of acceptance. (Chapters 13 and 14 will provide more about effective use of these two resources.) Drawing on these resources at appropriate times can let others know that it is perfectly all right for them to share their spiritual concerns with you.

Be Alert to Spiritual Needs

Creating an atmosphere of acceptance is a start, but you also need to be alert to detect spiritual needs, expressed or unexpressed. In a caring relationship an individual might never say one word about God, faith, or any other religious matter, but this does not imply that the person has no spiritual needs. It might simply reflect the nature of a society that tends to suppress spiritual matters. Being alert to what people feel and think (as well as what they say) is important. Your ability to discern the spiritual dimension in the life of a care receiver could result in answering a hidden cry for help from someone involved in a spiritual crisis.

Encourage People to Discuss Spiritual Needs

The author of Proverbs wrote: "The purpose in a man's mind is like deep water, but a man of understanding will draw it out" (20:5). Just as individuals need encouragement to express their feelings and needs in other areas of life, they also need encouragement to talk about their spiritual needs. When caring for someone, you will probably ask general questions like "How are you feeling?" or "How are things going?" or "What would you like to see happen in the future?" Similar questions can also be asked about the person's spiritual life. For example, you could inquire:

- "How is [a particular crisis] affecting your view of God and life?"
- "Do you see yourself as a religious or spiritual person?" (If the answer is yes, follow this up by an appropriate open-ended question.)
- "How do you see God fitting into your life?"
- "What values are important to you?

Another way to encourage people to share their spiritual needs is to ask specific open-ended questions. Unlike the general spiritually oriented questions above, the following questions are prompted by what the person is specifically experiencing. For example, you could say:

- "You mentioned that you have been experiencing a lot of suffering recently and that you are wondering if God could be punishing you. Could you elaborate on that?"
- "You say that you're frequently depressed since you have retired, that there's nothing left in life for you. It's almost as if you have lost your sense of purpose."

Sometimes after you say something to encourage a person to talk about the spiritual, the individual will answer with a religious cliché, or a general statement that does not really express how he or she is feeling inside. For example, the person might say, "God means everything for the best," or "I go to church every Sunday" or "Oh, I believe in God." None of these statements fully expresses how the person feels about his or her life in relationship to God. To move beyond clichés, you may need to ask some follow-up questions that allow the individual to explain his or her feelings in greater detail. Here is a sample excerpt from the middle of a conversation to show how this might be done, involving Mr. Adams mentioned earlier in this chapter.

Caregiver: You're facing some major surgery tomorrow, George. How are you feeling right now about God?

Mr. Adams: Oh, I don't know. I go to church every Sunday, you know.

Caregiver: You are very faithful in coming to church, and that's good. I'm wondering, though, how your relationship with God is affected by all this?

Mr. Adams: I guess God will be with me.

Caregiver: You say that God will be with you. Could you tell me more about what you mean?

Mr. Adams (*fidgeting*): Whether I live or die in surgery is out of my control. I believe God is in control and will do what is best. I have faith in him.

Caregiver: Would you like to talk to God about that, George? I'll be glad to join with you in a prayer.

Mr. Adams (*dispiritedly*): What difference would it make? God doesn't care what I want.

The caregiver has seen a small bit of the spiritual crisis Mr. Adams is undergoing and can work with him in it. The caregiver can continue to provide an atmosphere of acceptance and encouragement so that Mr. Adams can express his concerns and fears with the caregiver, and eventually with God.

Take Whatever Time Is Necessary for Extended Conversation about Spiritual Concerns

Occasionally, you and the other person might decide to discuss a single spiritual concern in greater depth. You might even spend an entire conversation focusing on a particular spiritual issue. For example, suppose you are talking with a man who knows he has cancer and might not have long to live. He told you that he has been struggling to understand his illness and probable death in light of his faith in God. Certainly you will want to spend a lot of time discussing his feelings and thoughts about his illness and his relationship with God. It is important that you take sufficient time to actively listen to him and to understand his faith struggles. Since this is a personal, sensitive matter, the man's anxiety and tension will probably intensify as he explores his feelings. By taking the time to listen, understand, and discuss, you can enable him to gain new insights into his relationship with God and new growth in his faith as he struggles with his situation.

Pitfalls to Avoid

By staying away from a few common pitfalls in ministering to someone's deep spiritual needs, you will significantly increase your effectiveness as a caring person.

Avoid One-Way Street Discussions

One of the dangers of discussing spiritual concerns is that the discussion can easily become a one-way flow of words from you to another person. You might have responded well to the needs and feelings of your friend until a spiritual question was raised. At that point you could be tempted to shift into the role of a lecturer. When this happens, the conversation quickly becomes a monolog in which you do all (or most) of the talking. The relationship is no longer between equals, but becomes that of a superior instructing an inferior. When relating to spiritual needs, the discussion should always be a dialog—a mutual exploration of religious feelings and needs. Talking about God or faith is not taking a funnel and pouring the right words into someone's head. It is a sharing process in which you will both speak and listen.

Avoid Religious Clichés

There are many religious clichés and pat phrases in common use. Be careful to avoid using them in your helping relationships. Examples are:

- "All you need is faith."
- "Praise the Lord anyway."
- "Don't worry, God loves you."

Although such clichés might contain some truth, in many contexts they are shallow, inappropriate responses to difficult life problems. Clichés frequently offer little insight and, furthermore, prevent both you and the other person from really speaking meaningfully and to the point. If you do not know what to say, it is better to say so than to resort to a pat religious phrase. When you do have something spiritual to say, don't use a cliché.

Avoid a Know-It-All Attitude

You no doubt have strong convictions about certain matters of faith. A problem can arise if you are tempted to act as the final authority on spiritual matters and try—perhaps even unwittingly—to force your convictions on others. A rigid attitude on your part can yield negative results in the caring relationship.

First, and perhaps worst, the person might passively buckle under to your conclusions, agreeing with you without thinking things through. Second, an attempt to force your views on someone could cause him or her to reject or avoid spiritual matters entirely. Third, trying to force your own understanding on someone could start an argument. This is certainly non-productive for spiritual growth. Feel free to share your insights, but there is no need for you always to justify your beliefs, or worse yet, force your own understandings on another person.

Everyone's life has a spiritual dimension. God persists in revealing this dimension wherever and whenever he can, despite society's continual efforts to thwart him. As one who seeks to care for others as a Christian, you need to be ready to relate to the deep spiritual needs of others. Your readiness to do so will be communicated to others by the climate of acceptance and encouragement you create, by your sensitivity to opportunities to raise the issue, and by your willingness to take whatever time is necessary. The person you are caring for will find you trustworthy because you do not respond with clichés or behave in a lofty, superior manner, and you listen as well as talk. Thus, the door will be open for providing care that is deeply and distinctively Christian.

8

Ministering to the Whole Person

"We did it first and we do it better!" Many companies originating a specific product have found a slogan like this to be a valuable selling point. They often advertise that their specialty "was there when it all started," "does it the old-fashioned way," "has lasted through thick and thin," and most importantly, is "the best." Christians can apply this phrase to their holistic approach to caring and relating to others.

Interest in holistic health, holistic care, holistic medicine, behavioral medicine, and the like has blossomed recently as many from the medical and scientific world have sought to understand and treat the whole person. I do not minimize these 20th-century developments in holism by secular specialists. However, a complete picture of the history of holism and holistic care must include the seminal teachings and practices of the Judeo-Christian tradition.

Jesus Christ taught and practiced a holistic approach 2000 years ago. Earlier, the Old Testament writers emphasized the unity of the person. Despite the unquestioned usefulness of modern secular holistic theories, it is clear that the biblical tradition "was there when the holistic thrust began," "does it the old-fashioned way," "has lasted through thick and thin," and can even make the audacious claim to be "the best!"

Holism and the Old Testament

Old Testament writers continually present a holistic view of the human being. The Hebrew understanding sees the person as a total being, without soul-mind-body divisions. To illustrate, I will treat three basic themes: creation, brokenness and healing, and the Hebrew concept of peace.

Creation

The account of Adam's creation is a good example of holism in the Old Testament. Genesis 2 states that God created Adam like a caring artisan, forming him from dust. God then breathed into his nostrils the breath of life, and Adam "became a living being" (Gen. 2:7). The picture of a statue-like corpse of a human, motionless and lifeless, suddenly gaining life and breath with personality, emotion, and coordinated movements is awe-inspiring. It also shows that the first person really was incomplete until the physical element was united with the breath of God.

Brokenness and Healing

In the Old Testament the person was viewed as a whole. Brokenness for the Hebrews meant spiritual, emotional, and physical brokenness all at once. The cause and result of all such brokenness was a broken relationship with God. Before healing could take place, the relationship with God had to be restored, or made whole. When the Hebrews were healed, they were made whole. There were no separate cures for the physical, spiritual, and emotional. Health was a divine, holistic gift.

Peace

The concept of peace provides even more insight into the Old Testament's holistic view. Peace conveyed the idea of wholeness in relationships, health, welfare, prosperity, and spirit—all of them. The Hebrew word *shalom*, used by Jews and adopted by many others today as a greeting, means "peace be with you" and is used for both "hello" and "good-bye." It connotes completeness. Old Testament peace occurred when things were as they should be in the eyes of God and in the world. The peaceful life is life as it was when God created the world, life in the Garden of Eden. There no barriers existed between God and people; complete harmony existed in every aspect of life. When you greet another with "shalom," you convey a blessing for a continued holistic life.

Holism in the New Testament

Jesus' Words

Jesus teaches a holistic approach to our relationships with God and others. Central to Jesus' teachings is love, which is to characterize all interactions. This love is not merely physical or emotional; it completely embraces the whole person.

Jesus teaches, "Love the Lord your God with all your heart, and with all your soul, and with all your mind" (Matt. 22:37). Jesus' teaching about love for God suggests complete devotion. Jesus breaks away from any distinctions in a person's nature, calling for complete, holistic dedication to God.

Jesus also teaches that relationships with others need to be holistic. Following the great commandment to love God with our whole being, Jesus says that we should love others as we love ourselves (Matt. 22:39). We can have holistic love for ourselves. We don't need to separate love for our spirits from love for our bodies. We don't need to separate love for our social being from love for our emotional being. We love our whole person.

Following Jesus' teaching involves meeting people where they are and treating them as Jesus Christ himself: feeding the hungry, giving drink to the thirsty, welcoming the stranger, clothing the naked, comforting the sick and visiting the imprisoned (Matt. 25:35-38). The parable of the good Samaritan emphasizes this concretely (Luke 10:29-37). The Samaritan first met the victim's immediate needs. Next, he took care of the man's future needs, providing him a place to stay and someone to take care of him. Such care is holistic because it meets the needs of the whole person.

Jesus' Actions

Jesus practiced what he preached, providing holistic care for all people. He met people at the point of their special needs, including their spiritual needs, because they were one and the same. On the way to raising the daughter of Jairus from the dead, a woman who suffered from severe bleeding for 12 years touched Jesus' robe. Instantly she was healed. In one action Jesus met both the needs of her body and her spirit. Her physical healing was stopping her flow of blood, and her spiritual healing was the gift of faith (cf. Luke 8:43-48).

A similar incident occurred when a paralyzed man was lowered through the roof into the room where Jesus was teaching. Jesus made the man spiritually whole by forgiving his sins and physically whole by healing his paralysis (Mark 2:1-12). In John 7:23 reference is made to Jesus' *holos* healing of a man on the Sabbath day. The use of *holos* with the noun *hygies*, meaning ''healing'' or ''soundness'' indicates that Jesus' healings are complete, permeating the entire person.

Many other actions of Jesus were holistic, each making a less-than-perfect person or situation whole. The feeding of the 5000, the healing of the 10 lepers, and the stilling of the storm are three examples. Even on the cross, suffering with a crown of thorns on his head, nails piercing his hands and feet, and the crowd mocking him, Jesus holistically reached out to touch his mother's brokenness by providing for her present and future needs (John 19:17-42).

Salvation in the New Testament

The salvation that Jesus brings to the world is his ultimate act of holism. Sin resulted in brokenness and separation from God. Fragmentation destroys families, friendships, and individuals. We erect walls that alienate ourselves from others and seal off hopes for reconciliation. Into the shattered remains of God's perfect creation comes the message that Jesus Christ brings the gift of wholeness to anyone able to accept it. It is the gift of salvation won by Christ's death and resurrection and received through faith that has torn down the separating wall of sin and restored our relationship with God. The Greek word for ''to save'' (*sodzo*) also means ''to heal'' and ''to make whole.'' It is a gift of life offering to make people whole forever, beginning right now. It is this salvation, this healing, that takes broken, shattered lives and recreates them infinitely ''better than new.''

Overabundance

Jesus abundantly offers wholeness to our world. In John 10:10, he says, ''I came that they may have life, and have it abundantly.'' There have been many translations of the Greek word *perisson* (to the full) in this text. I prefer translating the word "overabundantly" to express the unending, overflowing life that Jesus offers to his people.

Pitfalls in Being Holistic

When holism is misunderstood or misapplied, difficulties can arise for both the caregiver and care receiver. These pitfalls need to be avoided so as not to short-circuit the helping relationship.

The Splitting Pitfall

This pitfall is encountered when a caregiver attempts to split apart the person receiving care. For example, a caregiver who treats the spiritual separately from the physical and the emotional, has stumbled into this pitfall. An example is the caregiver who keeps all Scripture, prayer, and talk about God separated from the care receiver's personal problems. When this occurs, the spiritual has been split apart from the physical, emotional, and mental aspects of the person. As caregivers, we can also stumble into this splitting pitfall in dealing with ourselves. We can compartmentalize the various aspects of our own personhood. For instance, at one time we might let emotions dominate our behavior when we are extremely angry. At another time, we might let the spiritual part of us dominate, while suppressing physical or emotional needs. A holistic perspective unites all aspects of the person, while neither denying part of self nor artificially emphasizing some aspect of self.

The Ranking Pitfall

This includes the compartmentalized approach, but also involves setting the compartments against one another by ranking them. The tendency for us Christians might be to rank the spiritual nature over the mental, emotional, social, and physical. To call this ranking a pitfall is not to say that being spiritual is in any way wrong, since God wants your relationship with him to be foremost in your life. But we also need to remember that God does not simply want your spiritual self. He wants your heart, soul, and strength (Deut. 6:5). God wants your whole person because we *are* whole persons, not parts that rank one over the other.

The Perfectionistic Pitfall

The perfectionist pitfall is the most pernicious of all for Christians. Concentrating on the way life ought to be, we may continually strive for perfection. We might try to be all things to all people. We may want to be the infallible spouse, friend, neighbor, employer, employee, church member, or Christian caregiver. Many of us are seduced by perfectionism—seduced into thinking that since we *ought* to be perfect, we therefore *can* be perfect. Perfectionism then becomes the driving force in our lives.

As a Christian caregiver you need to realize that you cannot be all things to all people. Perfection is impossible. You are probably not a combined physician, business person, psychologist, teacher, farmer, provider of every need, all wrapped up into one. Neither can you be a perfect caregiver. Thinking along these lines all too easily leads to the perfectionist trap. Caught in the impossible mission of trying to make every aspect of your person and vocation perfect, you become dejected— even burned out—in your caring and relating.

The Self-Punitive Pitfall

There is no question that holistic thinking and treatment is therapeutic. Holistic treatment is successful. Its benefits are obvious. Because of its positive effect, some holistically oriented caregivers feel a tremendous responsibility for *their own* continued health and healing. Since they take the holistic approach seriously, they know that their own physical health is largely under their control. Therefore, when a disease like cancer strikes, there is the tendency to blame themselves for failing to be in touch with their whole person, for having too much stress, or for exposing themselves to carcinogens. And if healing does not take place, there is a further tendency to blame themselves for not holistically effecting a cure. This results in self-blame and guilt. These people become victims of the self-punitive pitfall.

It is important to understand the grace of God and the concept of forgiveness. When Christians stand under this comforting blanket, freely given to them out of love, the Christ of the cross shoulders the pain, the responsibility, and the consequences of the pitfall. Christians are free to live, care, and be cared for holistically.

Christian Caregiving Is Holistic

It ought to be clear by now that a Christian *must* be holistic. The Christian caregiver follows the example of Christ, who was holistic as he cared for others.

A Christian caring relationship meets people at the point of their unique needs, just as Christ himself did. A holistic Christian caregiver would not provide what would be considered spiritual care alone to someone in desperate need of food or water. Here, a specifically physical need, rather than a traditionally spiritual need must be satisfied immediately.

Abraham Maslow's hierarchy of needs illustrates how caregivers can recognize priorities in care. Maslow suggests that there are essential needs that must be met before the motivation to satisfy other needs arises. He formulates five levels of need: physiological needs, safety needs, belongingness and love needs, esteem needs, and self-actualization needs. Before one can be motivated for safety needs, basic physiological needs such as hunger, thirst, oxygen, and sleep must be met.

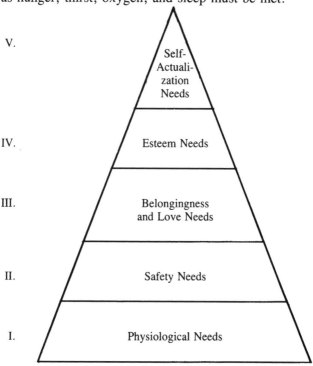

V.   Self-Actualization Needs

IV.   Esteem Needs

III.   Belongingness and Love Needs

II.   Safety Needs

I.   Physiological Needs

In this hierarchy, religion would be a self-actualization need, one of the higher needs for which one would be motivated. Thus, we see the importance of meeting persons at the point of their own need. That need must be fulfilled before purely spiritual motivation can exist. This is an essential part of holistic care.

A Christian caring relationship touches the whole person. It is not limited to the physical, or the mental, or the social, or the emotional, or the spiritual. Christian caregivers follow the example of Jesus Christ and cannot avoid being holistic to the best of their abilities. Christian caregivers understand that the whole person needs ministry. Christian caregivers realize that some needs are more immediately compelling than others. Christian caregivers know that God alone is the one who takes broken individuals and makes them whole.

9

Servanthood vs. Servitude

Martin Luther wrote, "A Christian is a perfectly free lord of all, subject to none. A Christian is a perfectly dutiful servant of all, subject to all."

You are called to freedom as a Christian—to freedom from the coercive obligation to serve and from irresponsible apathy, but more importantly, to the freedom to serve.

Few aspects of Christianity are more subject to misgivings and misunderstanding than the call to servanthood. Guilt, anger, and miscommunication are often associated with it—all traceable to a basic confusion of *servanthood* with *servitude*. *Servitude* connotes bondage, slavery, and involuntary labor. *Servanthood*, on the other hand, incorporates the ideas of willingness, choice, and voluntary commitment.

There is a world of difference between servanthood and servitude. At best, the person snared by servitude acts out of a sense of duty and fear, but the person living in servanthood acts out of a sense of commitment and love. Servanthood is healthy and uplifting, although involving challenges, pains, and problems. Servitude is, by definition, unhealthy and demeaning for all concerned. The net result is that servitude creates more difficulties than no service at all—both for the server and the one being served.

Christians sometimes have difficulty distinguishing between servanthood and servitude—mainly because of misreading certain passages of Scripture. As a result, we can feel enslaved to our calling rather than freed by it. Under these circumstances caregiving becomes an act of servitude.

A primary reason Christians become entangled in the web of servitude is the fear of not pleasing God enough. It is all too easy to fall into the mind-set that if I overdo in my service of caring for others, I will ingratiate myself with God, making up to him in one area what I might be lacking in others. To err in this direction is to misunderstand God and perhaps to injure the one I purport to help. By acting in servitude, I often depersonalize the care receiver, robbing him or her of individuality, responsibility, and motivation.

Some people believe that Christianity inevitably leads to servitude, or at least confuses the meaning of servanthood. I disagree. I believe the distinctiveness of Christianity helps to clarify true servanthood. Just as Christians can learn much from the secular sciences, so the secular world can learn much from Christians about servanthood. Secular individuals can also fall into the trap of servitude, on the one hand, and apathy, on the other. Christianity provides the way of escape from both of these traps.

Fantastic possibilities open up for us as Christians when we understand servanthood. If being a Christian servant is not easy—and it isn't—it can, nonetheless, be gratifying. With the guidance of the Holy Spirit, we can make the most of our servanthood, bearing in mind that we allow God to guide us. Without God's direction, we are headed for trouble.

In the following pages I will present four basic *servitude* problems and their corresponding *servanthood* responses. The following chart summarizes them. To be sure, there are many others, but these should provide a dynamic framework to help you discover and analyze the rest.

Servitude	Servanthood
Overidentification Taking on the problems of the other at the expense of losing your own identity	*Empathy* Feeling with the other while retaining a good measure of objectivity; maintaining your own identity
Superficial sweetness and gushiness Compensating for frustration or anger by covering up feelings	*Genuineness* Being yourself, wounds and all; acting congruently
Being Manipulated Allowing the other to abuse your relationship	*Meeting Needs, Not Wants* Being straightforward about your feelings, speaking the truth in love; confronting another when it is called for
Begrudging Care Complaining about your caregiving relationships	*Intentionality* Choosing to be in a caregiving relationship, or getting out of it when that is what is best for all concerned

Servitude Pitfall #1: Overidentification

When people experience problems in life, it is as though they are stuck in the mud. When you, a caring individual, relate to someone in such a plight, you can be tempted to jump into the mud in order to assist him or her out of the mudhole.

If you do this, you are overidentifying with the other person. That is, you reach a level of emotional entanglement at which the other's pains, problems, and emotional burdens become your own. It is true that you achieve emotional solidarity with the other, but look at what you lose. By jumping into the mudhole and becoming totally submerged in the other's problems, you forfeit the objectivity necessary to get the other person out (not to mention getting out yourself).

The result is that no one benefits. The other person is still in need of care, and now you need help as well. Misery does indeed love company, but misery needs more than company in order to be helped.

The Servanthood Approach: Empathy

Walking in the freedom of servanthood, a Christian responds to the other's plight with empathy. Empathy involves experiencing another's problems as if they were your own, without losing the "as-if-ness" aspect. It entails jumping into the mudhole with the other, but at the same time firmly grasping a tree root. That is, you retain your sense of objectivity.

When you empathize, the other person senses that you share his or her problems, but you have the all-important objectivity that enables you to communicate, "Let's get out of this together." With empathy you firmly grasp the other person's hand and help him or her through the quagmire back onto stable ground.

Servitude Pitfall #2: Superficial Sweetness and Gushiness

When someone claims to love everybody, my detectors tune in sharply, especially when the person demonstrates this love in an excessively sweet and gushy manner. To me this is often a good indication that the person is using what I like to call a "cover opposite." That is, a person reacts with incongruent behaviors that cover over—and are usually the exact opposite of—his or her true feelings. So the person who feels reluctant, unwilling, or maybe even angry at the prospect of serving cloaks that feeling with an exaggerated and unnatural sweetness.

This defense mechanism is a denial of one's humanness and brokenness. It can even be a form of self-righteousness. The sweet and gushy carer is out of touch with him or herself. He or she refuses to face the brokenness within, and often scorns the brokenness in others from some imagined height of spiritual maturity.

This situation is bondage. Individuals caught in its tenacious grasp are so deceived that they cannot see that anything has gone wrong with themselves. To be sure, people like this can be the first to grovel over the presence and power of sin in their lives. Yet it is evident that the groveling is only a mask for an attitude of superior spirituality.

So long as the caregiver is ensnared in this pitfall of superficial sweetness, no in-depth relating can take place. The one seeking help is only interacting with a mask, a facade.

The Servanthood Approach: Genuineness

The servanthood approach to others is not superficial sweetness and gushiness, but genuineness. Genuineness stems from being in congruence with yourself. It is being who you are.

Being genuine does not mean being perfect, but entails a recognition of brokenness in yourself. As you learn to recognize your brokenness and feel at home with it, you will be able to capitalize creatively on the imperfections in your life of caring. At these times God can be strong in your weakness.

Genuineness is disarmingly contagious. As you, the caregiver, learn to set aside the masks that society and your own imperfection continually thrust upon you, you will be an enabler and a model for others to do the same. A genuine caregiver's vulnerable openness at the point of his or her brokenness can indeed be an incentive for others to shed their masks and be themselves.

Genuine, congruent individuals are not liked by everyone. Sometimes others find it hard to like a person who, by being congruent, shatters their illusions. Perhaps the best example of this is Jesus. When he acted congruently, it aroused anger and hatred sufficient to lead to his crucifixion.

Sometimes you may feel that you are being "crucified." When you open up in a courageous act of caring by being genuine, not all will be appreciative. Some might resent your freedom. No matter. Your caring results from a deliberate decision to care in a given situation and to care through the pains and burdens that reveal your own brokenness. Being a servant is not easy, but the reward of spreading genuineness to others is worth the price.

Servitude Pitfall #3: Being Manipulated

Perfectly sincere, caring Christians have shown by their actions that they consider being manipulated to be honorable and Christlike. Being manipulated is a means of demonstrating their long-suffering endurance; it is part of the cross they are called on to bear.

Being manipulated is not Christian servanthood. In *The Manipulator and the Church* Dunnam, Herbertson, and Shostrom define a manipulator as "one who exploits, uses, and/or controls himself and others as things or objects." You are being manipulated when another person controls your behavior or plays on your emotions for selfish ends—treating you more as an object than a person. When you are manipulated, the relationship ceases to be meaningful. When you permit someone to treat you as an object, you block any genuine relating. A one-sided "relationship" in which the manipulator has all his or her whims fulfilled is no relationship at all.

Allowing yourself to be manipulated demeans yourself. When you let it happen, you are in effect saying, "Okay. I am an object. I am your plaything." Furthermore, when you permit manipulation, you allow the other person to demean his or her own self. You give your approval to the diminution of the individual's personhood. Far from following the apostolic injunction to "build one another up," you help the other person to tear himself or herself down.

A good example of the destruction that accompanies allowing manipulators to have their way is with the alcoholic. The phone calls made by a spouse to excuse an alcoholic's lateness or absence from work might seem rather loving acts. They are not. They do not help a chronically chemically dependent individual. Far from fostering growth, continually rescuing the alcoholic from self-imposed trouble only serves to reinforce behavioral patterns that are destructive for the alcoholic and the rest of the family.

The Servanthood Approach: Filling Needs, Not Wants

If you love people and seek to build them up, you must meet their needs, not their wants.

Being a true Christian servant involves not allowing yourself to be manipulated. It entails giving people what they need, which is not necessarily what they want. For example, a child might want six scoops of ice cream for dinner, but what the child needs is a balanced diet of meat, vegetables, and fruit.

The same goes for people—children or adults—who are manipulative. To pander to their whims is usually a good way to insure that their true needs will not be met. Certainly, you will keep their wants in mind. Many times, what people want will help them along the road of healthy growth. But to grant an individual's every whim is, almost invariably, to cultivate unhealthy, negative, and overly dependent behavior.

I do not mean to imply that you are excused from being warm, caring, and gentle with people. There must be time for nurturing in the caring process. But when the individual manipulates as a life pattern, you must not allow yourself to become another one of the person's toys.

Resisting this temptation will not be easy. You will need to learn skills of relating with and serving others. Returning to the example of the alcoholic, it will require you to be confrontive. The responsibility for being absent from work lies on no one's head but the alcoholic's, and he or she must not be permitted to shift the blame. Meeting the alcoholic's need entails helping him or her bear the responsibility for the action and admit, "I am an alcoholic." A direct, forthright approach is the only way I know to successfully combat manipulation.

Servitude Pitfall #4: Begrudging Care

Occasionally you can stumble into a relationship that you really did not want anything to do with. Yet, because you feel obliged to care, you continue in the situation—while at the same time constantly complaining about the individual and the relationship. If you find yourself in this predicament, you might seriously consider ending the situation, rather than continuing to participate grudgingly in it.

What I recommend here is not the same watery soup served up under the guise of, "If it feels good, do it," with its unspoken corollary, "If it feels bad, don't do it." I'm not saying that. At times you will experience great inconvenience and pain relating to another person, without the slightest urge to complain. Rather, you will find joy in bearing the burdens of another. But there are times when just the thought of associating with a certain person will fill you with bitterness and dread. In this case your resentment is probably blocking any effective relating and caring. Consequently, you might wish to reassess your involvement.

The Servanthood Approach: Intentionality

The individual who acts out of the freedom of servanthood will consciously choose to enter and remain in relationships. A deliberate decision to care lends power to your presence. Intentionality stands in stark contrast to unwilling care that results from a warped sense of obligation.

Even with intentionality, relationships will not always be sparkling and dynamic. Some relationships are more stimulating and rewarding than others. This could lead naturally to caregivers seeking out the more exciting relationships and shunning the less exciting ones. It is often easier to relate to attractive people than unattractive ones—especially when no deliberate decision was made in the first place. But when such a decision is made, the strength of your commitment will carry you through some exceedingly dull times.

This glorious gift called freedom that God gives in servanthood rules out rule-giving. Rather than requirements, what I offer are some guidelines. Learn them for the value they have, but also rely on the promptings of the Holy Spirit who gives you the gifts you need as a Christian servant. God does not give all gifts to all people. It follows that you cannot expect to be able to serve every person who is in need. Still, you need to use the gifts God *has* given you, recognizing both your strengths and your limitations.

You also need to beware of expecting others to have the same gifts you do. Do not judge those who are not involved in Christian service in the same way as you.

By God's grace, you can continue to grow in your servanthood attitudes and capabilities. A limitation today could become a strength tomorrow. God isn't finished with you yet. Accept your limitations; give the care you can. Some gifts you might never have.

Remember the example of Jesus. Distinctively Christian service takes its cue from the Lord himself, who willingly washed his disciples' feet—not as a demeaning task but as an act of selfless love (John 13:1-15). Christ defined servanthood when he said that "the Son of man came not to be served, but to serve, and to give his life as a ransom for many" (Matt. 20:28).

In *A Thousand Reasons for Living*, Dom Helder Camara summarized the difference between servanthood and servitude:

> Do people let you down?
> Don't carry them on your shoulders.
> Take them into your heart.

10

A Surprise Gift: Forgiveness

Human beings constantly fall short of God's expectations. All have faults, failings, and imperfections that repeatedly cause us to fall before God and say with the prodigal son, "Father, I have sinned against heaven and before you; I am no longer worthy to be called your son" (Luke 15:21). Because of this, one of the richest resources of the Christian faith is the surprising gift of forgiveness that God offers us through Jesus Christ. God freely offers forgiveness to everyone. Christians throughout the ages have found special comfort and renewed life in the promise of forgiveness.

God shares this message of forgiveness through his people. As members of the body of Christ, Christians have Jesus' command to extend God's gracious offer of forgiveness to one another (John 20:23). What a gift!

Not only do Christians have the assurance of forgiveness in God's written word, but God also puts the message of forgiveness into the hearts and mouths of people. At times when God's forgiveness seems foreign and remote, a warm human being will communicate God's forgiveness, helping me grasp more fully that God has truly forgiven *me*! Your ability to share the forgiveness of God with others is one of your most valuable assets.

The Nature of Forgiveness

Forgiveness makes the God-human relationship possible. If God's mercy had not triumphed over his justice, the only road open for humans would have been eternal punishment and separation from God. But for Christ's sake God forgives sinfulness and sins. The forgiven sinner is no longer held accountable for wrong done.

A great exchange took place. On the cross Jesus became our sin so that we can receive his righteousness. God's forgiveness is his pardon. As the psalmist proclaims, "As far as the east is from the west, so far does he remove our transgressions from us'" (Ps. 103:12).

It is the removal of sin through the sacrifice of Jesus Christ that restores and transforms divine-human relationships (and human-human relationships as well). Wrongdoing builds walls of alienation. God's forgiveness abolishes these walls and restores our relationship with him. Martin Luther King Jr. described forgiveness in this way:

> Forgiveness does not mean ignoring what has been done or putting a false label on an evil act. It means, rather, that the evil act no longer remains as a barrier to the relationship.

As well as being integral to our relationship with God, forgiveness also characterizes relationships with others. The ongoing process of forgiveness means continually putting aside all the obstacles between ourselves and others.

In this sense, forgiveness is an absolute prerequisite for caring. It is difficult to care for another without forgiving that person, removing the barriers in the relationship. You might believe that the person has done some very serious wrongs. Yet God calls on you to forgive that person and to demonstrate your willingness to forgive by accepting him or her.

Acting in a forgiving way does not require that the person first confess his or her sin to you. You can forgive "unilaterally." This provides an opportunity for healing to take place in the relationship. One powerful example of unilateral forgiveness is Stephen: "And he knelt down and cried with a loud voice, 'Lord, do not hold this sin against them.' And when he had said this, he fell asleep (Acts 7:60). Another is Jesus on the cross: "And Jesus said, 'Father, forgive them; for they know not what they do' '' (Luke 23:34).

This is not to say that confession of sins is unimportant. A healing word of forgiveness is meaningful only when the care receiver recognizes the need for forgiveness. So that the other person can truly receive what you have to say, be patient and listen with understanding before verbally offering forgiveness. Yet, from the outset, you can approach the person with a forgiving, accepting attitude that facilitates, without attempting to coerce, repentance.

The forgiveness you offer is distinct. Christian forgiveness is based on what Jesus earned on the cross and offers to everyone. It is forgiveness that restores people's relationship with God and provides new hope in their relationships with others. Thus, there is tremendous power and depth in the forgiveness you share with those weighed down by brokenness and guilt.

Offering Forgiveness

Here are some practical ways to introduce forgiveness into human relationships.

Acceptance

First of all, make forgiveness evident in your relationships by your acceptance of the care receiver. People need to sense that they do not have to meet any standards to earn your acceptance. One of the biggest problems we have today is that we are afraid to let others know who we really are. We are afraid to reveal feelings, sins, and imperfections to others because we fear rejection. This can also be true of our relationship with God. We are afraid to share our burdens of guilt with God, because we fear his punishment or rejection. If you expect others to open up and receive forgiveness, you need to communicate acceptance.

This is stated well in the words of the popular hymn "Amazing Grace." One line reads, "'Tis grace that taught my heart to fear." I understand this to mean that grace creates a situation in which my heart can honestly confront my inadequacy and fear. In other words, God's undeserved favor enables us to look at ourselves realistically (even though we might not like what we see).

Acceptance, also called unconditional positive regard, is vital in setting the stage for meaningful forgiveness to take place. By setting no conditions before caring, loving, and forgiving others, you avoid a condescending, moralistic attitude. A "holier than thou" attitude is not only un-Christian, but detrimental to a caring relationship. If you are shocked by something a person tells you, you may convey your natural shock, but be careful not to overdo it. Avoid acting in such a way that implies nonacceptance of the person. For example, suppose you are talking with a person who is 17 years old, pregnant, and unmarried.

She: I don't know how to say this, but I'm pregnant. What am I going to do? I feel so terrible, I wish I could die.
You: It sounds like you're upset by what has happened.
She: My life is a disaster. But the worst hasn't happened yet. I haven't told my parents. What are they going to say?

They'll disown me, reject me. You probably feel like rejecting me, too.

You: I am surprised about what you have told me—but I certainly don't reject you. I want to support you and help you work on this situation.

Communicating acceptance does not mean you overlook or approve of all the attitudes and actions of others. Rather, it means that you accept people in spite of their faults. For example, suppose a young person confesses to you: "I should never have lied to my parents. They're going to be badly hurt when they learn the truth."

Not helpful: Don't worry about it. I know you didn't mean to do it.

Helpful: Yes, it probably would have been better to be truthful from the start. I agree with you. Would you like to take some time to share your feelings and talk about what you might do now? I'm willing to listen and help you figure out what you might do next.

Listen First

When people need to unburden themselves from the guilt they carry around, take time to listen to what they are saying and feeling. One temptation that can get in the way of listening is the impatient desire to speak a forgiving word prematurely without hearing everything the other person is trying to say. You need to listen attentively before verbally sharing forgiveness. Only by listening fully to what people are thinking and feeling, and helping them to see the consequences of their actions, can you truly help bear the burdens of others.

When forgiveness is shared too quickly, it is rendered meaningless. Dietrich Bonhoeffer calls this "cheap grace." People need to come to terms with their guilt. Self-realization is necessary for change. Time is required for self-examination and confession. People must see their need for forgiveness; otherwise your declaration will seem irrelevant or impertinent. Either they will think, ''You cannot possibly forgive me! You don't know half the story!'' or they will think, ''Why is he or she forgiving me? What did I do wrong?'' Thus, for a person to experience forgiveness fully, sufficient time and accepting love need to be provided in the caring relationship.

Reporting on a training project in community mental health, Granger Westberg and Edgar Draper noted that clergy often do not take time to listen fully to people before sharing forgiveness. In *Community Psychiatry and the Clergyman*, they wrote:

> In fact, if we have had a problem with our project clergymen, it has been to get them to be firmer with people. Many are actually less effective in counseling because they want to declare God's love and forgiveness too soon in the counseling process. In most cases the people who come to them are not at all ready for such an absolution. They really have to work through their guilt and wrestle with their own ambivalence toward the guilt they feel and need to confess.

This does not mean you should *withhold* forgiveness from others. What is necessary is to take time to listen fully to others and help them unload their burdens of guilt, rejection, failure, and sin before you verbally forgive them.

Here's an abbreviated example of a conversation in which a friend takes time to listen fully and helps the other person face the reality of the situation:

He: My father died over a year ago, yet I still feel really guilty about our relationship. We had a lot of problems getting along. Two days before he died, I walked out on him during an argument. I never talked to him again. Then it was too late. How can I forgive myself?

Friend: Along with not getting along generally, your father died before you had an opportunity to make peace with him after an argument.

He: Yes. If I am reminded of him during the day, sometimes I won't even be able to sleep that night. I had so much love for him despite our difficulties. I should have told him so.

Friend: It must be very painful to talk about your relationship with your father as well as look at yourself at the same time.

He: I know it's too late to say anything to my dad— this side of heaven anyway. I suppose I should learn from my mistakes and forget about the guilt. What's done is done.

Friend: I'm not so sure it's all that easy. Although your father has died, I don't think you can just go on as if nothing happened. The point is that deep inside you feel torn up over the friction you and your dad had and not expressing your love to him before he died. As you said, there are some nights you can't even sleep. We might need to spend more time talking about it. What do you think?

He: Yes, I guess you're right. I hoped this thing would just go away, but it's probably something that I need to talk about more.

These statements are only a small part of the conversation. Notice that the friend did not rush in with a message of forgiveness and immediately say:

> That's okay. I understand how you feel. But it is important to remember that God forgives you and I forgive you, too. The past is wiped clean.

That's not forgiveness. Those are just cheap words because they come too quickly. In all probability, the individual would continue to feel burdened by his guilt feelings, since he would not have had the opportunity to get out how he really felt. Notice, instead, that the friend took time to listen and to point out to the son the reality of the situation, even when he was somewhat ambivalent about discussing it. And note that throughout the interchange, the friend showed complete acceptance. Acceptance and listening are integral to helping a troubled person receive forgiveness.

Speaking Words of Forgiveness

After listening to their feelings and allowing them to unburden themselves to you, you will want to share with them verbally the gospel message of forgiveness. How you share words of forgiveness depends on you, the other person, the situation, and the need. There are several ways to do it. You might want to share a brief statement or two about God's love for that individual on account of Christ in spite of his or her sin. You could say something like:

> I'm glad you were willing to talk about _____. I know it was painful to be so honest with yourself. I want you to know that God loves you and forgives you in spite of your mistakes. As a fellow Christian, I also want to assure you of my own forgiveness. You are a very special person to me.

Or, you could turn to a passage or story in the Bible that proclaims God's forgiveness and say something like:

> I know you are really having difficulty accepting the forgiveness that God offers. I find it is important for me to

remember that God accepts me for who I am, regardless of how I feel. The story of the prodigal son illustrates for me the forgiving love that God has for us. Would you like me to read that story to you? (cf. Luke 15:11-32).

Or perhaps:

Sometimes it is hard to believe that our sins could *ever* be forgiven. But God has given us his promise to be right there with us even when we find it most difficult to forgive ourselves. The Bible tells us, "If we confess our sins, he is faithful and just, and will forgive our sins and cleanse us from all unrighteousness" (1 John 1:9).

There is no more exciting or life-transforming news to share with people than that God has forgiven them. This news should be shared with care, listening to the person before speaking. Yet, if the need is there, you dare not omit words of forgiveness. Your responsibility to the care receiver is to provide the very best, and there is nothing better than forgiveness in Christ.

Forgiving Yourself

As a postscript to this chapter, I want to discuss the person most often neglected in the forgiveness process: you. In his book *The Wounded Healer*, Henri Nouwen clearly brings out the fact that we are part of a broken world. All suffer from wounds of loneliness and alienation, make mistakes, and have a variety of shortcomings. Yet Nouwen claims that our wounds can be turned into sources of healing as we recognize that pain and suffering come from the depth of the human condition, and that healing comes only when Christ enters those depths.

This means that being human is both your greatest resource and your greatest liability. You can be creative and spontaneous, and you can make mistakes. You can be empathic and caring, and you can be self-centered and inward-looking. What is important is to recognize and accept that you aren't perfect. It is only then that you honestly demonstrate humanness. When this takes place, the care receiver can better relate to you, because he or she will relate more easily to someone fully human, genuine, and honest. Also, you as a caregiver can be more relaxed and work more effectively when you aren't under the pressure to do everything perfectly.

Falling into the perfectionist trap can actually result in your focusing more on your own needs rather than those of the person you care for. You can become wrapped up in self-evaluation rather than in caring for others.

In order to avoid the dangers and pitfalls of perfectionism, you need to forgive yourself for the inevitable mistakes that you will make. You need to recognize your mistakes and short-comings for what they are. Yet the fact is that God has already forgiven you. You are free from your sins. You have a real basis for forgiving yourself: God has already done so.

11

Confession and Absolution over the Back Fence

Confession and *absolution* are religious terms often relegated to a reserved spot in the china cabinet of religious heirlooms, to be taken down and used only in a very formal way. But the concepts are much too useful just to let them sit around gathering dust.

Confession and absolution is the process whereby one person communicates the burden of his or her sin to another, and the other person, in turn, shares with the burdened individual the good news that God has forgiven the sin and promises to heal the brokenness. Whether the setting for confession and absolution is liturgical or nonliturgical, structured or unstructured, in a church or over the back fence, it is a valuable resource for Christian caring and relating.

Confession and absolution differs from what happens when a person confesses to God in private and receives forgiveness directly from him. Private confession and forgiveness between one's self and God is indispensible. Yet sometimes a real live human being assuring another that God has forgiven him or her can be a great comfort. Realizing that you are privileged to share God's absolution (forgiveness) in a personal, one-to-one context can increase the effectiveness of your caring. You are functioning as an ambassador of God, carrying the embassage of divine forgiveness to a broken world.

Before you look at confession and absolution in a distinctively Christian way, first consider it in a broader context. Something similar to confession and absolution occurs in secular caring, when someone bares his or her soul to a friend and is accepted and forgiven. Catharsis and acceptance in secular caring is certainly healthy but different from Christian confession and absolution.

Where does the distinctiveness of Christian confession and absolution lie? When the Christian caregiver speaks a word of absolution, he or she speaks with the full authority of God himself. The fact that the absolving is actually performed by Jesus Christ *through* the Christian caregiver distinguishes the absolution offered by you from that of a secular caregiver. When you offer absolution, you speak for God as well. The person who confessed to you cannot realistically respond, "So you accept and forgive me. What does that mean? You are only one person. Nobody else does." As a distinctively Christian caregiver you speak as the messenger of the great King.

As a Christian in a caring situation, you have a potent resource in the confession and absolution process. Speaking words of absolution constitutes a major part of acting as God's ambassador. But how is this done?

Proper Relationship between Confession and Absolution

To illustrate the proper relationship between confession and absolution, I want to share with you three examples of the confession and absolution process in the same situation. The first two examples are what you should *not* do. The third is an example of a proper relationship between confession and absolution. Bear in mind that these examples are somewhat exaggerated to illustrate a point, and that the dialogs are excerpts, abbreviated and summarized from those likely to occur in actual situations.

In the following examples, a man called Jim has recently gone through a divorce. About a month before the divorce was final, Jim's children spent the weekend at his apartment. He spent the entire time unjustly criticizing and undermining his wife in front of the children. The result was that since then the children have been disrespectful and disobedient to their mother. It is now four months later, and after reflecting on his actions and receiving a phone call or two from his baffled ex-wife, Jim is feeling realistic guilt over his actions. In looking for someone to talk to about this, he turns to three of his Christian friends.

Harsh Harry

The first friend he approaches is Harsh Harry.

Jim: Say, Harry, do you have a couple of minutes?

Harry: Sure, Jim. What's on your mind?

Jim: You know about my divorce, Harry, and—well, there's something that's really been bothering me.

Harry: What's that, Jim?

Jim: A month or so before the divorce was final, I had the kids over for the weekend. I must have spent the entire time criticizing Madeline to the kids. I said some stuff that was exaggerated and not true. As a result, they have become quite disrespectful toward her. I just don't know what to say.

Harry: Well, you'd better find out what to say—to those poor kids and then to God. You were wrong, you know that, don't you?

Jim: Yes, I know. I'm really beside myself. When I heard from my wife, I mean my ex-wife, and she said: "What did you *do* to those kids?" I—

Harry (breaking in): Well, I don't blame her.

Jim: The kids have been rather disobedient to her and very disrespectful. I'm afraid I created a monster.

Harry: I think you have too.

Jim: I guess I am looking for some help from you as a friend and as a Christian. I just don't know what to do.

Harry: I don't think I can offer you anything until you realize what you've done.

Jim: I—I think I do. I'm really sorry for doing it. I really wish it wouldn't have happened.

Harry: Have you asked God for forgiveness?

Jim: Well, yes and no. I feel so bad and so ashamed. I don't think I know how to.

Harry: I think you had better do just that. You need to pray for enough grace to reconcile yourself with them and with God. He will forgive you.

(The conversation goes on.)

Although it may appear otherwise on the surface, Harsh Harry is not allowing any *real* confession to take place. Harsh Harry deals in superficiality. The bottom line for Harry is getting Jim to use some magic words like "I repent." He makes forgiveness dependent on words correctly spoken, while neglecting the inner struggle Jim is undergoing.

One danger of Harry's heavy-handed approach is that Jim might give in to Harry just to get him off his back. That would be unfortunate, because Jim would be pretending to have feelings that really were not his. At best, Jim's "repentance" would be external, not a matter of the heart.

Another danger is that Harsh Harry might make Jim feel bombarded and defensive, causing him to run for cover. Were this to occur, Jim might be driven to justify behavior of which he is inwardly ashamed.

Libertine Larry

The second person Jim talks to is Libertine Larry.

Jim: Say, Larry, do you have a couple of minutes?

Larry: Sure, Jim. What's on your mind?

Jim: You know about my divorce, Larry, and—well, there's something that's really been bothering me.

Larry: What's that, Jim?

Jim: Well, a month or so before the divorce was final the kids came over for the weekend. I spent the entire time running down Madeline to the kids. I said a number of things that just weren't true. I feel awful.

Larry: Oh, I can understand how you would say things like that. You were really upset at the time. I wouldn't dwell on it though.

Jim: But I talked to Madeline, and she said I created a monster. I have to agree with her. Since that weekend, the kids have been really disobedient and disrespectful to her because of what I said.

Larry: You know how kids blow things out of proportion. The kids are probably trying to manipulate her. I wouldn't buy the whole story she gave you. Besides, that's in the past. You've got to look to the future.

Jim: Yes, but I know that I said some very untrue and harmful things. I exaggerated some things about her.

Larry: Okay, so you made a mistake. I think that was just a normal reaction on your part, don't you? It's just overcompensating for what you've gone through. You're being too hard on yourself.

Jim: Well—maybe—but, some things I really did to an excess that weekend.

Larry: I suppose we could debate for a long time whether what you did was in excess. Even so, the kids will heal. Kids are tough. They bounce back. What's done is done.

Jim: I guess—

Larry: Besides as Christians, we need to remember that God forgives us our sins, and you are certainly forgiven for what happened.

Jim: I guess so—

(*The conversation continues.*)

Libertine Larry demonstrates one of the major pitfalls in many caring relationships. He did not allow Jim to fully express the *realistic* guilt feelings he was having. He did not allow any real confession to take place at all. Jim brought Larry a garbage pail that was once shiny and new, but is now filled with refuse. Instead of helping Jim empty out the garbage and then clean the inside with a word of absolution, Larry took some cheap perfume and sprayed it on top of the garbage in the can. Jim would leave his encounter with Larry carrying a superficially sweet-smelling can, still full of garbage. Larry erred by giving premature absolution.

Caring Cary

The third person Jim speaks with is Caring Cary.

Jim: Say, Cary, do you have a couple of minutes?

Cary: Sure, Jim. What's on your mind?

Jim: You know about my divorce, Cary, and—well, there's something that's really been bothering me.

Cary: What's that, Jim?

Jim: Here's the story. I've just got to tell someone. I picked up the kids about a month before the divorce was final, and they stayed the weekend with me. I spent the entire time running down Madeline to them. I told them things about her that weren't true and blew other things out of proportion. One bad word led to another—

Cary: You couldn't resist the initial temptation. Then once it started, you couldn't stop.

Jim: Exactly. And the worst part is that since then, they have become very disrespectful toward Madeline. You know, I was really unfair to her. Those kids actually believed me!

Cary: You really see yourself causing this.

Jim: Yes. I realize that as Christians we're forgiven for things like this, but what I did—I'm not usually like this. I don't like to hurt people. I certainly don't want to destroy Madeline's effectiveness with the children. It's she who will be doing most of the child rearing. I want to support her.

Cary: You're feeling bad, angry at yourself. You know what you did was not right.

Jim: Yes, but maybe I'm being too hard on myself. After all, what's done is done.

Cary: I don't think it's all that simple, Jim. I don't think you can simply pretend nothing happened and live happily ever after.

Jim (after some silence): You're right. I was only fooling myself. I really messed things up. I just don't know where to turn, what to do.

Cary: Jim, have you said anything to God about all this?

Jim: Yes, I told him I was sorry. I told him I had acted wrongly and thoughtlessly.

Cary: Do you believe that he has forgiven you?

Jim: I guess so. I'm having a little trouble really accepting that, though.

Cary: It's hard for you to accept forgiveness for this thing you did—even God's.

Jim: Yes. I bet he thinks I'm terrible. I bet you do too.

Cary: Wrong, yes. Terrible, no. I certainly forgive you, and I know God does as well. You know and I know that was a foolhardy and sinful thing you did, but that's what God forgives—sins.

(*The conversation continues with Jim and Cary later on talking about what Jim might do to rectify the situation with his children and ex-wife.*)

Caring Cary is characterized by *balance*. He was willing to sit down with Jim and hear him out. He did not run when Jim started to empty his garbage pail. Cary realized that Jim had already started doing his own confessing and did not need to take over and push Jim into a stylized confession. Note that when Jim started to drift into rationalization, maybe to avoid confronting his own guilt, Cary gently and firmly led Jim back onto the track of real confession. Although definitely caring, Cary was certainly not "easy."

In terms of facilitating a confession that was not superficial, Cary's approach was the best and most lasting of the three. By not rushing in too quickly with a word of absolution and short-circuiting Jim's confession, Cary demonstrated that he really cared how Jim was feeling. He felt no need to clutter up the conversation with timeworn clichés or hunting for magical formulas. Caring Cary demonstrated the proper relationship between confession and absolution.

12

Tools of Your Trade: Their Use and Abuse

Imagine yourself in this situation:

Someone very dear to you has died. You are beyond the initial shock stage of your grief and are hoping someone will help you work through your sorrow and find meaning in your life. Though you might not think it in so many words, what you want is some specifically Christian care. You are well-acquainted with two persons in your congregation and are open to their help and comfort.

One of the caregivers, Eric, comes to visit you. Among other things, you want to talk about your doubts and struggles related to your faith in this time of grief, and you tell Eric so. Eric, however, gives you no opportunity to elaborate on this. He expresses sincere concern about your grief, but disappoints you by failing to help you look at the meaning of your faith in this time of crisis. Although you continue to mention your spiritual struggles, Eric ignores this. Finally, when it comes time for him to leave, you ask Eric to have a prayer with you. In somewhat embarrassed fashion, he responds by stumbling through an abbreviated, woodenly constructed prayer, which makes you feel uneasy. And as Eric walks out the door, you feel unfulfilled and empty inside.

A few days later, Brenda, the other caregiver from your congregation, comes to visit. You still want Christian care for your grief. But before you are able to begin expressing your feelings, Brenda starts sharing Bible quotations and her views on the doctrine of the resurrection with you. Without giving you a chance to say how you feel inside, Brenda recites a well-rehearsed dissertation on how the sting of death has been done away with in Jesus Christ. And finally, before leaving, Brenda tells you to get down on your knees with her and then goes through a general prayer on death and resurrection that has no reference to your personal needs. You are somewhat embarrassed, hurt, and angered by this whole scene, and you are greatly relieved when Brenda walks out the door.

Although he expressed natural human concern over your experience of sorrow, Eric offered you nothing distinctively Christian in his visit. Despite the fact that you communicated to Eric your need for distinctively Christian care, he offered you none. Brenda, on the other hand, demonstrated knowledge about some unique resources of the faith, but she did not employ them in a sensitive or helpful way. Brenda disregarded you as a human being by using Bible verses, doctrine, and prayer without reference to your personal, individual needs. She used them as tools to maintain control of the caring situation. Both Eric and Brenda left you without effective holistic Christian care.

In your caring situations, formal or informal, you need to avoid the two extremes illustrated in the caricatures of Eric and Brenda. You need not feel reluctant to use the unique resources of the faith, such as praying with someone, sharing a Bible passage, talking about God, and perhaps ending visits with a blessing. You do need to avoid bombarding individuals with Christian resources without regard for their unique situations and needs.

You might determine that it is inappropriate to be overtly Christian in your helping in some situations of human need. There is much caring that a Christian can do without outwardly using Christian resources. That's all right. You don't have to use traditional resources if the situation doesn't demand it, or if it seems unnatural to talk explicitly about religion at times. However, if a situation of need occurs in which a person could be aided by sharing the resources of the faith, by all means use these resources.

Freedom to Use Christian Resources

For various reasons you might, like Eric, feel reluctant or afraid to use the Christian resources at your disposal. Here are three reasons why you can feel free to be truly Christian in your helping.

Not for Pastors Only

Some might think that it is up to ordained individuals alone to meet the so-called spiritual or religious needs of people and to be the only ones to use the traditional resources of the faith. This is simply not true. The "universal priesthood of all believers" is a fundamental Christian concept. Again and again the Bible states that every Christian, regardless of his or her station in life, shares with all other Christians the privileges and responsibilities of the faith. See, for example, Exod. 19:6; 1 Peter 2:4-10; Rev. 1:5-6; 5:9-10; 20:6.

Whether you are clergy or laity, you need to take this notion of "universal priesthood" with utter seriousness. All Christians need to put their priesthood into action—ministering to each other and to the rest of the world. You have the resources of Christianity available for your use in helping and caring situations. So do not hesitate to use these resources.

The Tools of Your Calling

Another reason you may feel free to use Christian resources is that they are the tools of your trade. Whether you are clergy or not, you are a priest, a minister. You have the right to claim with confidence the privilege of using these tools to exercise fully your distinctive type of caring. When a physician uses a tongue depressor, scalpel, or stethoscope, it doesn't seem strange. Similarly, when a dentist uses Novocaine, dental floss, or an X-ray machine, you don't consider that inappropriate. In the same way, you, a Christian caregiver, need not be reluctant to use the tools of your profession. Tools such as prayer, the Bible, talking about God, blessings, and the like are often appropriate and healthy ways to care for and relate to others. To ignore the traditional resources of Christianity in a caring situation would be much like a physician choosing not to use medical equipment during surgery.

Others Expect You to Offer Something Different

Caregivers who do not profess Christianity often recognize the Christian approach to caregiving as valid, and some even esteem it highly. Knowing this can free you to use your unique tools of caring. Of course, if others do not show respect for the distinctiveness of the faith, it is still important to witness to it, indeed to *be* it. But the fact is that even many helping professionals—physicians and psychologists, for example— expect Christians, ordained and laity alike, to offer people in need something different from what they are able to offer.

During my internship in clinical psychology, a group of psychologists, psychiatrists, interns, and residents met weekly over a brown-bag lunch at what was called a Journal Club. For an hour each Wednesday noon, we discussed various journal articles and recent research findings. Occasionally we would invite a guest speaker from the medical center to discuss his or her work. One Wednesday, a local chaplain was invited to speak. During the course of his presentation, he was asked by one of the therapists what distinctive or unique elements he brought to the healing endeavor. The chaplain responded that he thought he could give a distinctive type of help by offering more long-term types of counseling, because he didn't have to rotate his clients as much as the mental health personnel. When someone asked the chaplain whether he used prayer, Scripture, and other Christian resources as part of his distinctive approach, the chaplain responded, "Well, that's really not my bag."

The psychologists and psychiatrists at the meeting were outraged, amused and full of pity. Their attitude seemed to be: "This chaplain offers nothing distinctive in the helping process. What he does, we can do better. He's just getting in our way if he offers nothing uniquely 'religious' to people." Many secular professional helpers, even those who aren't Christian, recognize and indeed respect the distinctively Christian way of helping.

Incidentally, secular professional helpers aren't the only ones to recognize and respect Christian uniqueness; so do many other people. Even non-Christians expect you to use religious resources as you care for people who are of the faith. Although non-Christians do not necessarily want Christian resources applied to their own needs, they do respect Christians who use prayer or Scripture in the course of helping and relating to others.

It is true that Christianity has a bad name for some people. Sometimes the hostility of secular professionals and others can even be merited. But such situations are rare. The more you show your distinctiveness appropriately, genuinely, and effectively, the more other people will respect you for who you are and what you stand for—even if they do not believe as you do.

Guiding Principles

There are two guiding principles to follow when employing Christianity's distinctive resources.

Don't Treat People as Objects

Avoid treating another as an object, as territory to be captured rather than someone respected in his or her own right. Some display a spiritual imperialism that seems concerned only with converting people to their own religious views rather than helping individual people of God become whole. Treating people as objects, as territory to be gained, is not only bad manners, but also completely fails to meet their unique needs and to respect their spiritual dignity before God.

Now, there are many ways—some quite subtle—of treating a person as an object. For example, you could become so concerned about getting your own religious ideas across to the person with whom you talk that you forget there is an individual before you with unique problems that need to be ministered to. You also might be preoccupied with getting in Bible readings and prayers, forgetting that an individual might need these resources tailored to his or her own situation. Or you might be in such a hurry to share your faith with someone that you neglect to notice the person is not yet ready to hear your testimony.

Questions you always need to ask yourself are these: *Am I here to help the other person, or am I here to help myself, to further my own goals? Am I using the tools of Christian helping to fulfill my own needs or the needs of the other person?* If your words and your actions show that you have no ulterior motives for relating to someone, and you are interested solely in helping the person with his or her own unique needs—then you will avoid ministering to him or her as an object.

Match Resources to Needs

Effective caring entails listening skills to discover the person's needs and life situation *before* you do anything else in the helping relationship. You must always be sensitive to each individual's situation, what the person's needs are, before you use any traditional tools for Christianity. You need to listen attentively and explore an individual's frame of reference before you can minister effectively to that person.

You have the privilege, the right, and the responsibility to be distinctively Christian when you relate to and care for others. The resources at your disposal are not to be ignored; neither should they be used inappropriately. Learn to use them sensitively and effectively.

13

Prayer

Prayer is supposed to be matter-of-fact for Christians, taken for granted as part of the faith environment. Yet it remains one of the most difficult resources to use appropriately and effectively in caring relationships. This is true for clergy and laity alike, but especially for lay people. Many believe that praying with someone is a right limited to clergy. Nothing could be further from the truth. It is every Christian's right and responsibility to pray with others as the opportunity arises.

A major reason people are reluctant to pray with others is their uncertainty as to how to go about it. They are unsure about why they should pray with others, when to pray, how to pray, what to pray about, and even where to pray.

While the focus of this chapter will be the use of prayer in more-or-less structured caring visits, much of this material will apply to everyday encounters with others. I hope this chapter will reaffirm your existing skills and suggest new ways to use prayer in caring situations.

Why Pray with Others

God invites his people to draw near and share their concerns with him by means of prayer. God also specifically invites his people to approach him in prayer together. James 5:16 urges

"Pray for one another." The context clearly shows that the reference is to two or more people praying together.

Not only do we pray for each other because God urged it; we also pray together because Jesus added his special promises to shared prayer:

> Again I say to you, if two of you agree on earth about anything they ask, it will be done for them by my Father in heaven. For where two or three are gathered in my name, there am I in the midst of them (Matt. 18:19-20).

What a powerful incentive to pray together! When you pray with another, God is the third party in a caring relationship, actively concerned for you and for the person with whom you are praying. In prayer God has promised to listen to you attentively, to understand your needs, and to answer your requests. Thus, your motivation for praying with others extends far beyond the fulfillment of a religious formality.

Another reason for mutual prayer is the beneficial effects on your relationship with the other person. Consider what an intimate personal experience prayer is. As you are honest with the God "from whom no secrets are hid," you are also honest and open with each other. As you draw nearer to God, you will naturally draw closer to each other.

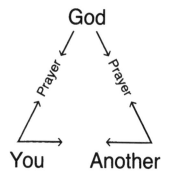

Intimacy that grows as a result of joint prayer, is intimacy seldom experienced in contemporary society.

Jesus said:

> But when you pray, go into your room and shut the door and pray to your Father who is in secret; and your Father who sees in secret will reward you (Matt. 6:6).

Some people think this means that prayer always needs to be very private and personal, taking place only between God and the person. The context shows that Jesus is warning against false piety, not against praying together. He is warning people against parading their religiosity for others to see. Your purpose in praying with others is very different. You are sharing their burdens and involving God in the process.

When to Pray

When It's Natural

Prayer should come as a natural part of a total visit. Because prayer cannot be programmed beforehand, you need to determine the proper moment to pray. That judgment depends on the other person's needs, not yours. In other words, don't pray when *you* are ready to pray, but when the *other person* is ready. Careful listening will help you ascertain when prayer is appropriate. Your goal is for prayer to be a natural part of your conversation, not an intrusion or interruption.

Not as an Injection

Prayer should not be tacked on to a visit artifically. It is not an injection enabling you suddenly to bring in the Christian viewpoint. If a visit has not demonstrated Christian concern up to that point, prayer will not magically make it Christian.

If for some reason you do not include a prayer, this does not mean that your visit is not distinctively Christian. Whether you pray or not, your entire visit must reflect Christian distinctiveness through your love and care for the other person. When you pray, it needs to be part of a total Christian visit.

Not as a Technique for Leaving

Although it is common practice to close a visit with prayer, you occasionally might want to pray with people at times other than the end of a visit. Prayer is not a technique for closing a visit. There are obvious and better ways to close such as:

- "Good-bye, I enjoyed talking with you today."
- "How about if we get together again."
- "I need to go now."

A danger of always closing with prayer is that the individual you visit might come to look on the prayer as a way to say good-bye rather than communication with God. The person might feel disappointed when you mention prayer, because it signals that you will be leaving. Remember that prayer can come appropriately at any time during a visit.

Not to Manipulate

There is always the danger that prayer might be used as a means of manipulating another into action that you want to see happen. If you want someone to join a choir, a manipulative prayer might go as follows:

Heavenly Father, I come before you today asking that you would bring about a change of heart in Mary, so that she would become willing to join the choir.

This prayer is merely an attempt to force the person's hand by arousing feelings of guilt. A prayer of this sort will probably have negative results. If the other person expresses a desire to pray for a change of heart on some matter, that's different. Then, the prayer is coming from the expressed needs of the other person, not your own hidden needs.

How to Pray

Introducing Prayer

Initiating prayer is awkward for some people. What do you say when you sense that prayer is appropriate? You might want to avoid a simple declaration like, "Let us pray." You might say something like:

● "Would you appreciate a prayer right now?"
● "We have talked about this problem and you have expressed a lot of feelings. Would you like to share these with God in prayer?"
● "You have set a personal goal for yourself. Would you like to pray about it, asking God for his help?"
● "I'm really glad things have gone well with you this week. Shall we share our thanks with God in prayer?"

These introductions leave the individual with a choice. Prayer needs to be a willing response if it is to be true prayer.

When the Person Says No

Most of the time, when you ask someone if he or she would like to pray, your suggestion will be welcome. Of course, the person can also say no. On those occasions, he or she will usually give a reason.

One reason could be that the person has already prayed extensively about the matter. If this is the case, remember that prayer should be based on the other person's needs, not yours.

Another reason could be that the person feels unworthy to pray. For example, while talking to someone who is going through a bitter and painful divorce, you suggest prayer. The person replies, "I'm too ashamed to pray. I don't think God will listen to me." Your temptation might be to brush off the person's feelings, saying: "God is a very gracious God, you know. And he is very forgiving, so there is nothing wrong with praying. Let's pray."

Don't do it! Give the person a chance to talk about his or her feelings. A better response might be: "You are so ashamed that you don't think God will listen. How are you feeling right now? I'm willing to listen."

The first response could pressure the person into doing something uncomfortable and unhelpful. The second response shows genuine concern and willingness to relate to the other's feelings. The individual might feel more open to prayer later.

Sometimes people say no to prayer because they don't like to pray. Although you have excellent reasons why prayer is beneficial, you can't force another to value prayer in the same way. To force prayer on someone can achieve opposite results from those you intend.

People could also say no to prayer because they prefer to pray privately and are reluctant to pray with someone else. While you need to respect their feelings, you might want to explain gently the benefits and joys of praying together. However, the final decision on whether or not to pray is theirs.

Whatever reason people have for saying no to prayer, you need not become defensive, nor think that you are being rejected. Moreover, as your relationship develops there might be other occasions when the person will feel more open to prayer. Be patient.

Addressing God

In prayer of any kind, you begin by addressing God. But what kind of God are you inviting into the relationship? Remember that God invites you to address him as your loving Father. Remember—and let your prayers show it—that God is a loving God who involves himself in the lives of his people. Jesus Christ, God's Son, became a human being and shared in all of human experience. He truly understands all of what you talk about when you pray to him.

Honesty

Do not avoid the pain and apparent injustice of a situation. Some people think they have to "clean up" their thoughts when they talk to God. To them feelings like anger, sadness, bitterness, or fear have no place in prayer. Consequently, they end up being dishonest with God. Martin Luther's first rule of prayer is "Don't lie to God." Feel free to share all emotions and experiences with God. God is loving and understanding and wants honesty from us, not prettied-up piety. Note how honestly Habakkuk cries to God:

> O Lord, how long shall I cry for help, and thou wilt not hear? Or cry to thee "Violence!" and thou wilt not save? Why dost thou make me see wrongs and look upon trouble? Destruction and violence are before me; strife and contention arise. So the law is slacked and justice never goes forth (Hab. 1:2-4).

Yet the prophet goes on to say: "God, the Lord, is my strength; he makes my feet like hinds' feet, he makes me tread upon my high places" (Hab. 3:19).

It is only by sharing painful moments honestly with God that people find themselves able to be helped.

Choosing Meaningful Words

Be sensitive to the needs and expectations of the person you are with. Choose language that the other person understands and with which he or she is comfortable. While the age of the person can affect your choice of words, you need not use language you are unfamiliar with, like slang with a teenager if you are an adult. Rather, choose words that are natural for both of you. You might want to avoid religious expressions such as "meet, right, and salutary" or "expurgate." You may also want to avoid the use of "thee," "thy," and "thou" unless that is more comfortable for you and the other person.

It is possible to be excessively critical of language or style. If you find yourself stumbling along and groping for words, keep going. Neither God nor others are concerned with eloquent words, only that genuine communication takes place. Paul wrote: "For we do not know how to pray as we ought, but the Spirit himself intercedes for us with sighs too deep for words" (Rom. 8:26). Many times the best prayer is the one most difficult to express, coming from the heart and reflecting genuine concern. As John Bunyan said, "In prayer it is better to have a heart without words than words without a heart."

What to Pray About

Pray about the person's need that suggested prayer in the first place. This prevents vague prayer and renders it more meaningful for the other person. Both you and the other person will benefit if you are clear about the need you will bring to God before you pray. How do you do this? Here is one way to ensure that both you and the other person understand what needs will be included in prayer:

> You are visiting Mrs. Thompson, who is facing surgery the next morning. Mrs. Thompson tells you she is worried and afraid. After listening to her, you ask if she would like to pray, and she says yes. You might say at this point, "In our prayer we'll be asking God to protect you in surgery tomorrow, as well as to help you with your worries and fears. Is there anything else you would like to express in this prayer?"
>
> When you say this, Mrs. Thompson could either respond: "No. All I want is God to be with me tomorrow."
>
> Or she might say: "Yes. Could we also include my family? I know they are very worried."

On the basis of either response, you can begin to pray, confident that it will speak to her real needs.

Building a Prayer

One prayer process I have found helpful is building a prayer. Building a prayer simply means that you and the person discuss what needs to go in the prayer before you start to pray. As you build a prayer, you discover the needs of the individual by asking open-ended questions, enabling the person to express his or her real concerns. For example, let's revisit Mrs. Thompson, who is facing surgery. Your conversation might go something like this:

You: Before we pray, what are some of your thoughts and feelings right now?

Mrs. T.: I'm worried that after surgery is over, I won't be able to take care of my children. I feel so alone right now.

You: You'd like us to pray about your fears of loneliness and your worries that something might happen tomorrow that would prevent you from being a good mother to your children?

Mrs. T.: Yes. I know I shouldn't feel this way and think these thoughts, but what if I die?

You: It sounds as if we should ask God to help you as you struggle with this fear of death. Is there anything else you would like to share with God in prayer?

Mrs. T.: No, these are my chief concerns.

By inviting Mrs. Thompson to share her concerns, you have information to use in building a prayer which meets her needs.

When Someone Asks You to Pray

On occasion another person might request a prayer. You might be tempted to immediately fold your hands and begin praying. But remember that prayer should meet the other person's needs—no matter who suggests it. A good response might be something like: "I would be glad to pray with you. Before I do, I'd like you to share with me what you're thinking about and what your needs are at this time. I think we could share them better with God that way." This is not an evasion technique, but a way to provide better quality ministry.

Using Prayers Written by Others

Although most of the praying I have talked about so far is extemporaneous, you could also choose to use a prayer book in your caring. Here are some specific suggestions for the use of prayers from books or other resources:

● Become well-acquainted with the prayer book you will use. This enables you to choose appropriate prayers quickly without paging through the book while the person is waiting.

● Choose prayers that meet the needs of the individual.

● If the person's need is of a nature that the printed prayer speaks to it generally or incompletely, add a sentence or two that is more specific.

● Read the prayer in a natural voice and at your normal rate. There is no need to switch to a dramatic, "stained glass" voice. A change in tone might distance you from the other person, adding an impersonal quality to the prayer.

● The Psalms are a "prayer book within the Bible." Again, become familiar enough with them through study and your own personal meditation that you can choose a psalm appropriate to a person's need without fumbling around.

● The Lord's Prayer is always appropriate, either by itself, or with another prayer. One of its advantages is that the other person can join you.

Where to Pray

You can pray with a person anywhere, provided you adjust your style of prayer to the surroundings. When a visit is in a private home, the setting is usually conducive to quiet moments of prayer. But prayers can also be appropriate in public places like a hospital. If you are with someone in a waiting room, however, you might want to postpone prayer or move to a place with fewer distractions.

Even in a patient's room, there is not always total privacy. If another patient is in an adjoining bed, you might want to adjust your style by praying more softly with the person you are visiting. Or, depending on the other person's religious orientation, you might want to include him or her in the prayer. Be sensitive so as not to bully other people into being included when they do not want to be. Remember also that the person you are visiting can be in such a state of crisis, pain, or sickness that he or she really needs your undivided attention. Don't dilute your ministry to someone who really needs your intensive care at that moment.

Prayer is our response to God's gracious invitation. It is based on the needs of the other person, confidently expecting God to act. As you go about being a distinctively caring Christian, both you and the person for whom you pray will find strength and assurance, knowing that your concerns are left in the hands of God, who is love.

14

The Bible

Many of the guidelines for prayer covered in Chapter 13 also apply to the use of the Bible in caring relationships. For example, as with prayer, your use of the Bible needs to fit in as a natural part of your total conversation. Just as you need to choose prayers to meet the specific needs of a person, so should you gear the sharing of biblical principles and passages to people's specific needs. There are two additional points to make, namely *why* and *how* you can use the Bible effectively in your caring relationships.

Why Use the Bible

The Bible is an excellent resource for ministering to people because it records how God has ministered to the needs of people through the ages. It is a written witness of the facts surrounding the "Strange and Marvelous Case of the Persistent Lover."

The Bible relates how God sent his Son Jesus to become a human being so that he could bring love, healing, hope, forgiveness, and new life to the world. The Bible summarizes the work of Jesus, saying, "For God so loved the world that he gave his only Son, that whoever believes in him should not perish but have eternal life (John 3:16)." The people you care for are people experiencing the bad news of the world. They live in the midst of suffering, oppression, conflict, grief, sickness, tragedy, and finally death itself. They could use some good news; they could use the gospel.

The Bible addresses itself to a broad range of human concerns, experiences, and situations. People frequently turn to Scripture, especially when they are experiencing problems and needs. The Bible contains reassuring words and promises of God. The Psalms, for example, run the gamut of human emotions from despair to exhilaration, from anger at God to love for him. The parables capture various truths that enrich the spiritual lives of people. The lives of biblical characters provide examples of people with weaknesses and strengths who placed their faith in God. The teachings of the Bible instruct people in the art of living in relationship to God and one another.

Therefore, you use the written Word of God because it contains the message people need to hear. You use the written Word of God because it is practical: it deals with the same kinds of concerns people still have. But there's a third reason to use the Word of God: it's alive! To paraphrase St. Augustine: "What the Scriptures say, God says." The Word of God works in the hearts of believers for good.

This is not to suggest that you should administer the Bible in large doses at every opportunity. A physician with a good drug does not prescribe it for every illness. You listen, you diagnose, and you use the Bible as a resource when it is appropriate.

How to Use the Bible Effectively

Choosing a Translation

The Bible translation you decide to use in your ministry will depend on your personal preference and perhaps your denominational background. Sometimes people you care for will feel more comfortable with a certain translation, and in such instances you might want to honor their preference. For example, Psalm 23 can lose significance for some people when it is read in a contemporary version. But there are also times when a good modern translation breathes fresh meaning into Scripture for someone. If you know which version an individual prefers, bring it with you, or ask permission to use the person's Bible.

Carrying a Bible

If you carry a Bible with you, it is a good idea to mark appropriate passages ahead of time with a slip of paper so you won't have to thumb around frantically trying to find a passage. A smaller sized Bible might be the best to use, one you can slip into your pocket or purse. A large Bible can create the impression that you came to bludgeon the other person into insensibility with a flurry of verses. If you do carry a larger Bible, keep it at your side rather than setting it down between you and the other person. In this way it will not interfere with the conversation, yet will be handy when you're ready to use it.

Knowing Passages Ahead of Time

In order to use the Bible effectively, it is important to know passages relevant to some typical situations. You can begin by keeping a list of appropriate passages as you do your own reading and collect verses from others. You might ask the people you care for if any verses are especially significant for them. That will not only equip you to be a better caregiver to them, but also will allow them to give you something.

Knowing some passages beforehand enables you to choose appropriate ones quickly and easily, matching them to the needs of the person. You might want to mark some of these passages in your Bible, or commit them to memory.

Introducing Scripture

When you think it would be helpful to refer to Scripture, you might say:

• When you talk about your feelings of sorrow, I remember the words Jesus spoke about people who mourned when he said, "Blessed are those who mourn, for they shall be comforted" (Matt. 5:4).

• Something that really spoke to me when I was in a situation similar to yours is the story of the death of Lazarus where it says, "Jesus wept." If it was all right for Jesus to cry with grief, it is certainly all right for us to do the same.

• You mentioned in the past that you enjoy reading the Psalms. Would you like to read Psalm 121 with me? I find that this psalm encourages me in personal difficulties, and maybe it will you too. What it says is that God is always with you and is your protector.

What should you say after sharing a selection from the Bible with someone? Sometimes no further comment is necessary, since a passage might have spoken clearly and directly to the person's need. Other times you might wish to share a few of your thoughts about the passage and how it relates to an individual. Or you can simply ask the person, "Does this spark any thoughts or feelings in you that you'd like to share?" Be open to discussion.

Sometimes you and the other person will want to spend time discussing a passage. It is not a waste of time to spend much of a visit talking about one or more biblical selections if these center around the needs of the individual. In this kind of discussion, avoid extensive monologs. As you talk about a passage, be sure you do a lot of listening. This will help ensure that your discussion meets the needs of the other person. Your comments about the passage should guide the person toward understanding it relative to his or her own life situation.

The Bible is not to be used to lambaste, manipulate, or bombard people with your own judgments. Instead, share the Bible with them to bring reassurance, to confront when necessary, to deepen understanding, and to strengthen their relationship with God in the midst of their current situation. Your use of the Bible is another way in which your kind of caregiving—Christian caregiving—is unique.

15

Sharing a Blessing

In Chapter 13 I noted that you might not always want to use prayer for ending a visit. In the Judeo-Christian tradition, however, there is another distinctive technique that more aptly applies to such occasions—a blessing or benediction.

The Latin root of *benediction* simply means "well-saying." In this sense, benedictions also abound in the secular world. "Have a good day," people say. "Take it easy." "Keep your chin up." These are all benedictions of a sort. When taking leave, they are ways of wishing that all might go well with the other. One of the more commonly used "benedictions" has religious roots. To say "good-bye" is to use a contracted form of "God be with you."

There is an important difference, however, between secular benedictions and religious ones. "Take it easy," "Hang in there," and "Keep your chin up" all imply action on the part of the person to whom the farewell is extended, as though that person were responsible for the day going well. Christian benedictions, on the other hand, contain no such demand. They are professions of faith that the outcome of the day is in the hands of God. God's action is the foundation of the Christian benediction: "The *Lord* bless you . . ." "The grace of our *Lord Jesus Christ* . . ." "The peace of *God* . . . ."

These are all expressions of grace. God blesses you; you don't bless you. A benediction proclaims that God has you in his care and is responsible for your well-being. In this sense, benedictions are *remembering* tools. They remind the bestower and the recipient alike that God is present and he is in charge. Christian benedictions carry greater impact and bring comfort because you are acting in God's stead, assuring people that God will continue to be at their side. In offering a benediction you can make the presence of God even more real to the other person. In essence, you are saying, "I am leaving you, but you are not left."

How to Bless

Just as timing is important when praying or using Scripture, so it is important when you deliver God's blessing. Most often, blessings or benedictions will be appropriate at the close of a visit, but you might decide that a blessing is called for in the middle of the visit or at some other time. There might be other times when you determine that a blessing is inappropriate. Ask yourself: What is the other person's need? Would a blessing be appreciated and natural at this time?

When you decide it might be appropriate to use a benediction, you could lead into it by saying, "Before I go, if you like, I would like to share a blessing with you."

As you share blessings with people, physical touch can be important. You can grasp the person's hand or put your hand on an arm. Your touch can be a natural expression of the intimacy the two of you share at that moment as you stand before God, ready to receive the gift of his care. Touch is especially beneficial for those whose other senses might be handicapped—the aged, the infirm, the comatose, or the heavily sedated. If you feel stiff and awkward with touch, though, you might be better off not doing it. Your reluctance could be sensed by the other and detract from the blessing.

The Form of the Blessing

You have a broad range of options as to the specific benediction you use, and your choice can vary from one situation to another. As an aid in using this resource, you might want to write out one or more benedictions before a visit. Mark them in your Bible if you carry one, or better still, memorize several. You can be formal or informal in your choice of benedictions. Use whatever is appropriate.

Formal, stylized benedictions have their advantages. For instance, the familiar words of ''The Lord bless you and keep you . . .'' can be a great comfort to the person who has heard them week after week at the close of worship services. Here is a sampling of some of the more formal biblical benedictions you might find opportunities to use:

● The Lord bless you and keep you: The Lord make his face to shine upon you, and be gracious to you: The Lord lift up his countenance upon you, and give you peace (Num. 6:24-26).

● The grace of the Lord Jesus Christ and the love of God and the fellowship of the Holy Spirit be with you all (2 Cor. 13:14).

● And the peace of God, which passes all understanding, will keep your hearts and your minds in Christ Jesus (Phil. 4:7).

● Now may the God of peace who brought again from the dead our Lord Jesus, the great shepherd of the sheep, by the blood of the eternal covenant, equip you with everything good that you may do his will, working in you that which is pleasing in his sight, through Jesus Christ; to whom be glory forever and ever. Amen (Heb. 13:20-21).

Informal or extemporaneous benedictions are also appropriate and have their own advantages. If you are a layperson, you might feel uncomfortable using a formal, liturgical benediction. And if a caring situation happens to take place over a cup of coffee in a restaurant, a formal benediction could seem a bit out of place. Informal benedictions can be tailored to special needs and at times might even be more meaningful. For example:

Charlotte, may God shower you with his blessings as you begin your new job out of town, and may a sense of his presence be with you always.

Shorter blessings occasionally can be appropriate as well:

God be with you.
God bless you.
Peace and joy to you.

Speak these as seriously as you would the more formal or lengthy blessings, rather than in a casual or flip manner.

The situation, the person's needs, and your own preference will determine your choice of benediction. Whether you decide to be formal or informal, speak with conviction. Benedictions are not casual good-byes said halfway out the door, nor should they serve as stiff punctuations or formulas with which to conveniently conclude a visit. When you yourself are assured that the person really is in the hands of God, that assurance will come across in the blessing you speak.

Now I would like to share with you one of my favorite benedictions, one that appeals to me because of its holistic emphasis. I ask this for you now:

May the God of peace himself sanctify you wholly; and may your spirit and soul and body be kept sound and blameless at the coming of our Lord Jesus Christ. He who calls you is faithful, and he will do it (1 Thess. 5:23-24).

16

A Cup of Cold Water

It happened on one of those perfect June days that poets chatter about. My trip was successful, and business was finished well ahead of schedule. I was elated about the beautiful day, my additional free time, and the overall success of the trip. I decided to alter my travel plans and take the Old River Road.

Hours flew by and I soaked in the deepening blue of the sky and the dancing sunlight on the fresh green leaves as I drove on. To my right, the river flowed peacefully. Occasionally, I could see boats and people fishing along the banks. I ate a light supper at a quaint old inn along the roadside overlooking the river.

Pulling back onto the road, I saw that the beauty of the day was crowned with a glowing sunset. As the first stars began twinkling faintly in the purplish sky, I rounded a bend in the road and was brought to an abrupt halt.

Red lights flashed and a trooper, flare in hand, was motioning me off to the side of the road. Two cars had collided and their wreckage totally blocked the way. One, an old Buick, lay on its top and the other had rolled over at least once but had landed right side up. The scene was terrible. I began to regret having taken the back road when a trooper walked over and said to me, "There's been a bad wreck, sir. You'll just have to sit tight till the wrecker gets here."

Off on the far side of the road, I noticed a shape totally covered by a blanket. "Oh, God," I thought. "Why do things like this have to happen?" About 10 feet from the blanketed shape lay a man. He wasn't getting much attention because the troopers were busy making sure that no one else would come flying around the corner, adding yet another victim to the tragedy.

I got out of my car and crossed the road. The injured man was an older gentleman, wearing a suit. A slight trickle of blood ran from his mouth and when his eyes met mine, they seemed to plead: "Help me." I knelt down, unsure of what to do. He was obviously in pain. I quietly introduced myself and noticed that the trooper's jacket the old man was using as a pillow had slipped out from under his head. As I repositioned his head on the jacket, he mentioned his name was John.

The old man's eyes brimmed with tears as he told me what had happened. I listened. After talking for a while, he said, "You're very kind."

I quietly thanked him and smiled. No other words were necessary.

After a few moments he added, "I'm scared."

I grasped his hand and said, "I'll stay here with you."

The twilight had faded and night was approaching. John began to have some trouble breathing. "Could you loosen my tie?" he gasped.

"Of course. I'm sorry. I should have done that before."

As I loosened his tie and unbuttoned his top button, a small silver crucifix slipped out.

"You wear a cross. You're a Christian?" I said.

John smiled a painful smile and replied, "Yes, I am."

"Me too," I said, smiling back.

After exchanging a few more words about the faith we shared, I asked him if he would like for me to pray with him. He answered affirmatively. We talked for a few moments about what he wanted to include in the prayer. Many of his concerns were obvious. All I had to do was look around. There were some key items, however, that I was glad he made specific mention of, because I would not have included them otherwise. We prayed. God's love seemed to envelop us both.

As I was sharing with John my favorite verses from Psalm 139, the sound of an ambulance grew in the distance. Simultaneously, a car pulled up behind mine and a man and woman ran over to us. It was John's sister and brother-in-law. As they left together in the ambulance, I prayed: "Lord, go with them."

The Value of a Cup of Cold Water

Nearing home later that night, I began to reflect. When did my caring for John first become distinctively Christian? Was it when I shared the Psalm? When we first prayed together? When I first saw and commented on his cross? No. My caring was distinctively Christian from the time I first got out of the car, crossed the road, and began talking to John. Before I used a single explicit Christian resource, I was already manifesting distinctively Christian care.

God's supportive presence makes every aspect of your caring relationships distinctively Christian from the start. Jesus calls these actions of love flowing from God's promptings "cups of cold water."

And whoever gives to one of these little ones even a cup of cold water because he is a disciple, truly, I say to you, he shall not lose his reward (Matt. 10:42).

Explicit God-talk might or might not accompany these actions, but they are nonetheless vital aspects of total Christian care.

To be sure, when you pray, speak words of forgiveness, and talk about God, you are being distinctively Christian. But that's only one part of the picture. Any time you act out of God's love, whatever form your caring takes, you are also being distinctively Christian.

Jesus Christ does not stand on the sidelines waiting for us to use the right signal words for him to step in and be there. Rather, he is already in the middle of the situation. He's only waiting for us to see that.

The distinction frequently drawn between sacred and secular is more destructive than beneficial. It is just one way humans try to keep God boxed up and out of their everyday affairs. But God refuses to be put into any sacred boxes. He claims *all* of life—also the ''secular''—to be his own.

Exploding into every inch of our lives, God makes all of life sacred. This is the idea underlying this chapter: whatever caring you give or relating you do—even on days other than Sunday and in any life situation—that caring and relating is, by virtue of whose you are, distinctively Christian.

The Umbrella of Caring

I like to envision the entirety of Christian caring as an umbrella. That umbrella covers such things as prayer, talk about God, using the Bible, and ''cups of cold water.'' Giving a cup of cold water is not subservient or superior to any of the other more explicit Christian resources. It is part and parcel of Christian care.

Resources like prayer and Bible reading are important, but giving a cup of cold water is important as well. It is not an either/or proposition. It is a case of *both* a cup of cold water *and* traditional, explicit resources. Both are distinctively Christian tools. Both have their place.

The person who attempts to minister to others without appropriately using traditional resources is like a person trying to swim with one or both arms tied behind one's back. And conversely, the person who only uses traditional resources and consistently neglects the cup of cold water is left with only a caricature of true Christian ministry. Anyone who makes this an either/or proposition necessarily offers less than complete Christian care.

17

The Evangelism–Caring Connection

The word *evangelism* arouses mixed emotions among Christians. For some it represents the positive, forward thrust of sharing God's love, perhaps accompanied by a growing Christian community. But others have the impression that only preachy, fanatical Christians engage in evangelism. I am convinced that *evangelism* should evoke nothing but positive reactions and attitudes.

Evangelism is the act of bringing good news to someone. Originally, it had the connotation of bringing news of a battle won or of a fallen enemy. It is the action of one who witnesses a victory, and then runs to tell others about it. So, evangelism is the communication of good news that you yourself have witnessed to others.

Christian evangelism is communicating the surprising and beautiful fact that God truly loves us, and that he showed it by winning the victory over sin and death through the death and resurrection of his Son. God calls us to share the gospel message with all people. Just as I am called by God to be a Christian caregiver, so I am also called to evangelize. But I need to look at how I evangelize, how I communicate this good news. True Christian evangelism is caring; distinctively Christian caring is one vital aspect of evangelism.

Evangelism Is Caring

Evangelism is caring because the message I proclaim is the most precious message I possess. What greater gift could I share with others than love and life in Jesus Christ? Indeed, when I witness to what Jesus Christ has done for me—and all people—I show that I truly care about them. I show interest in their present and future.

Evangelism is also caring because the gospel of Jesus Christ is shared person to person. A true Christian witness is not a computer spewing out a canned message to people in general. He or she is a warm human being who has been personally touched by God's redeeming love and is now personally touching others.

The statement that evangelism is caring has a number of important implications.

● *Love is a vital motive for evangelism*. I need to be continually evaluating what leads me to witness for Christ. Am I simply interested in putting another notch on my spiritual gun or gaining members for my church? Am I concerned about the total life— the total Christian life—of the person to whom I am witnessing? St. Paul writes, "If I speak in the tongues of men and of angels, but have not love, I am a noisy gong or a clanging cymbal" (1 Cor. 13:1). One might read it this way: "If I speak all the right words of evangelism, but have not love, I am only making a lot of noise." If my evangelism is to be effective, my emphasis must be on caring for the person. This does not mean that numbers are unimportant. Growing church membership and attendance can indicate that effective evangelism is taking place. Yet my starting point is a message to and with an individual person who needs to be loved.

● *Evangelism is dialog, not monolog.* If I care about some-one, I will want to listen to that person. I will want to find out what that person is thinking, feeling, believing, and ex-periencing. I have a message to share, but before I can share it effectively, I need to hear the other person. What I say (or don't say) needs to be based on what I hear. This is amply illustrated throughout the New Testament. It explains why Je-sus proclaimed the good news differently to Nicodemus (John 3) than he did to the Samaritan woman (John 4). Evangelism as dialog is also evident throughout Acts. Consider the inter-action going on between Philip and the Ethiopian eunuch (Acts 8) and the way Peter relates to Cornelius and his household (Acts 10). If my evangelism is not dialog, my words are worth-less.

● *Good evangelism communicates God's love.* It is all too easy for me to set up false standards to judge the success of my evangelism. For example, it is tempting to play the numbers game, to see how many people I can superficially corral. What I must remember, however, is that I need to communicate my message of God's love to the depth of people's lives, because it is there that the Holy Spirit creates faith. I cannot do this through superficial contacts. Time must be invested in people's lives. It takes a good deal of self-sacrifice, an essential part of love.

Bearing all this in mind, I also discover from Scripture that there are limitations to my responsibility in evangelism. God told the prophet Ezekiel:

Son of man, I have made you a watchman for the house of Israel; whenever you hear a word from my mouth, you shall give them warning from me. If I say to the wicked, "You shall surely die," and you give him no warning, nor speak to warn the wicked from his wicked way, in order to save his life, that wicked man shall die in his iniquity; but his blood I will require at your hand. But if you warn the wicked, and he does not turn from his wickedness, or from his wicked way, he shall die in his iniquity; but you will have saved your life (Ezek. 3:17-19).

If I am a diligent watcher, if I have spoken and concretely demonstrated the love of God to another, and if in spite of all that, the other will not receive the love of God, then I have done all I can. I have communicated God's love, and good evangelism has taken place. The criterion for good evangelism is my communicating God's love as best I can, regardless of whether the other person receives it.

Caring Is Evangelism

If evangelism is caring, is caring evangelism? At first glance, it might not seem so. Actions of caring might appear to be quite removed from the work of evangelism. Certainly many people show love and concern in this world. Many who care are not Christian. Those who are Christian might not be identified as such. Thus, caring in and of itself might not seem on the surface to witness to the love of Jesus Christ.

But holistic caring is always evangelistic. Caring for another person involves meeting the needs of that whole person. Through actions of love, God reaches down and touches people with his power. His healing activity can renew all aspects of an individual's life. I am wrong if I try to limit God to what I might define as "spiritual." My caring provides a channel through which God's love can flow. My words and actions of love concretely demonstrate the good news.

This is particularly true of a good caring relationship. A quality Christian caring relationship is a concrete embodiment of the gospel, a model for the love that God wishes to communicate to people. It is God's mercy and grace that can now show forth in my relationships as I serve others, as I go the extra mile, as I go beyond justice and give of myself to those in need (1 John 4:7-16).

As I do this, I "incarnate" and thus demonstrate the Christian message. Through my caring I make the Christian message become something to hear about and something to be seen and touched. Through my actions I give flesh and bones to God's good news.

Caring is evangelism when in an imperfect world I actively live Jesus Christ. This does not mean that words are unimportant, but what I say and what I do must never be separated. Together they constitute a dynamic whole the Holy Spirit can use to transform the attitudes and beliefs of people, helping them to be made whole themselves.

An evangelism-caring connection works! Caring, evangelistic churches become magnets that draw and keep people. People want to discover the source of the love they experience there. They want to find out what makes their Christian friends so special.

Good evangelism and good caring are inseparable; each embodies the other. Evangelism shows forth a love for people, and a love for people shows forth the good news of Jesus Christ. This evangelism-caring connection presents an enormous challenge to me as a Christian. The work of evangelism-caring/ caring-evangelism cannot be accomplished if I restrict myself to my ecclesiastical ghetto, or if I speak the gospel without being the gospel. I need to get out into the world where people desperately need the love of Jesus Christ. So do you. May the Lord enable us to get on with the task at hand.

18

Celebrating Results

Helping people work through critical periods in their lives or resolve problems is rewarding. When you are involved in caring for another, it feels good to say: "I'm glad I was able to support Jennie during her time of grief. She's beginning to invest herself in living again." Or, "Tonight Arnie has finally accepted the fact he's going to die and is at peace about it."

To discuss results in a book about distinctively Christian caring is risky, because it might reinforce the tendency to focus excessively on results. Americans especially are characterized as result-oriented people. This attitude hinders caring. Focusing on results can be nonproductive—or even counterproductive—for both caregivers and care receivers alike.

Many of my clients in psychotherapy are basically oriented toward results when they first enter into therapy. One of my tasks as caregiver, especially at the beginning, is to help people toward a correct perspective on results. This is your task as well.

Overemphasis on results is so common that it's worth proclaiming as a rule: *results start happening when you stop pushing for them*!

Goals are helpful, and when Christians care for each other, good things do happen. Yet, as I have stressed throughout the book, your main focus as a caring individual needs to be on the *process* of caring rather than on results.

Process Goals vs. Results Goals

Process goals differ from *results goals* as verbs differ from nouns. Kindling a fire is a process; a fire is a result.

Suppose you befriend Jennie, whose spouse has died. You hope that through your caring relationship with Jennie she will recover from grief and get back on her feet. You realize that Jennie will adjust eventually, but through your caring ministry you hope she will work through her grief quickly and effectively. These are admirable ends, and ones that most anyone in the position of helping a grief-stricken person would desire. In your ministry to Jennie, you could focus on the *process* of caring for her or the *results* of caring. The effects of focusing directly on *results* could slow down growth and healing, or even prevent it.

What might be some *process goals* vs. *results goals* for Jennie?

Process Goals	Results Goals
1. Providing a comforting and accepting situation; helping Jennie talk openly about her husband's death.	1. That Jennie would no longer feel her loss as a raw wound, untouchable and excruciatingly painful.
2. Helping Jennie to express her feelings of sadness, hurt, or anger.	2. That although Jennie still mourns, her anger would dissipate and her sadness no longer incapacitate her.

3. Relating to Jennie in a caring and consistent fashion.

3. That Jennie would know that you care for her; she would trust you and begin to trust others as well.

4. Encouraging Jennie to share with you her fears about returning to her job and how she will handle offers of sympathy.

4. That Jennie would return to her job and successfully deal with people's offers of sympathy.

5. Helping Jennie to consider the possibility of entering into social situations.

5. That Jennie would get out, socialize, and participate in church and community activities.

6. Communicating to Jennie that it is both acceptable and healthy to grieve.

6. That Jennie would work through her grief.

Note that each of the process goals begins with a verb. Every one of them implies the passage of time. All of the results goals are beneficial, but each comes at the end of a process. You can't have an outcome without going through a process. And if you have your eye on the outcome, you probably will miss the process altogether.

Many an athletic team has failed because the players were thinking about the championship game while they were still playing the quarter-finals. When they lost that game, out went their chance for the championship. The good coach does all he or she can to direct the players to focus only on the game at hand and do their best job playing one game at a time. Even in a single game, the coach who excels will try to keep players' attention from the final score. The focus needs to be on the many actions that make up a good game: for example, basketball requires good dribbling, good passing, playing tight defense, and making baskets. Victories are results of many actions well executed; or in other words, victories come as a result of *process*.

Theological Implications

The issue of *process* orientation vs. *result* orientation is a difficult one to resolve by examining the Bible. The Scriptures do speak about results. As God works in your life, things happen. Through faith in Jesus Christ, you experience new birth. The apostle Paul says that "the old has passed away, behold, the new has come" (2 Cor. 5:17). The characteristics of newness in Christ include a relationship with God, the forgiveness of sins, the ability to lead a God-pleasing life, the experience of greater peace and joy, and day-by-day trust in God's guidance and protection. The apostle goes so far as to say that God "has blessed us in Christ with every spiritual blessing in the heavenly places" (Eph. 1:3). These are fantastic results!

For the Christian, results are primarily what *God* accomplishes. Yet God wants you to be a responsible individual, properly using what he has given you. He puts goals in front of you to work toward. Paul states, "I press on toward the goal for the prize of the upward call of God in Christ Jesus" (Phil. 3:14).

These considerations would seem to make you result-oriented, focusing on what God has done and will do for you and through you. However, the fact that God has given you goals implies that you haven't arrived yet. God has made us his saints, yet we remain sinners, people who do not always live in accordance with his will. We are always in need of spiritual growth and renewal. And so Scripture directs us to the *process* of Christian living:

> Work out your own salvation with fear and trembling (Phil. 2:12).
>
> Be transformed by the renewal of your mind (Rom. 12:2).
>
> Let all that you do be done in love (1 Cor. 16:14).

All the while you are engaged in the *process*, you work under the promise that "he who began a good work in you will bring it to completion at the day of Jesus Christ" (Phil. 1:6). For the Christian, therefore, *process* is intimately involved with *results*.

We live in a sinful world with its pains, illness, deprivation, and tragedy. As Job discovered, walking with God will not always entail pleasant feelings or financial success. God has not promised us a rose garden, a paradise on earth. We find ourselves within a troubled world—trying to spread God's love to individuals, institutions, and society as a whole. Being the "salt of the earth" is a continuous process.

The theology of process and results has several implications. First of all, you rely upon God for results. Ultimately all results in helping relationships are in his hands. He decides the nature and extent of the healing. You are called to trust in him and in his living providence.

Second, because you realize that God is the one who will provide healing in the future, you can focus more fully on the present. Jesus tells all Christians: "Therefore do not be anxious about tomorrow, for tomorrow will be anxious for itself" (Matt. 6:34). Given the assurance of God's loving presence and healing power, you are free to give yourself completely to the caring process.

Third, you can truly view yourself as an instrument of God, a part of God's process of healing. This provides a foundation of identity for the person giving Christian care.

Distinctive Results

What follows are some distinctively Christian results that can develop through the caring process. They may not all happen, but some will.

Community

Through receiving Christian care, a person can develop stronger ties with a community of Christians. As the person becomes actively involved with a fellowship of faith, he or she begins to feel a closeness to that community. Inner barriers and blockages—emotional, spiritual, personal—to other people are destroyed as the individual becomes more receptive to the warmth of the Spirit-given unity of that group.

Perspective on Suffering

Through Christian care an individual could better grasp the role of suffering in life. The person will be able to handle more realistically those problems and pitfalls that befall everyone because of the human condition. This will not totally remove pain, hurt, or anger, but the person will be able to look at suffering and handle it from a more mature perspective, with greater realism.

Forgiveableness

Forgivableness does not mean that people have somehow become worthy of forgiveness, but rather that they are able to *accept* forgiveness and grace from God and others. They will be more open to God's love, especially as it flows through others. In short, people will have learned to *receive*.

Forgiveability

A person receiving care might develop in turn the ability to give forgiveness and love. This often follows the acceptance of forgiveness or love, simply because it is impossible to give what one has not first received. "We love, because he first loved us" (1 John 4:19).

Trust

According to psychologist Erik Erikson, trust is an integral part of the first developmental crisis people undergo at an early age. Lack of trust is endemic in a society where broken relationships abound and people are almost expected to take advantage of you. As a result of Christian caring, a person might develop an overall increased level of trust, which can be foundational for other growth in the fullness of Jesus Christ. Who better is there to trust in?

A New Relationship with God

Christian caring leads a person to trust in the love of God. Through distinctively Christian caring and relating, a person who has not had faith in Jesus Christ can come to faith and experience the joy of Christian rebirth. God, working through his Word and the caregiver, creates trust in the care receiver. A person can be "born from above" through your caring and relating.

A Renewed Relationship with God

We all fall short of God's will for us. When we fall, it can be a long time before we permit God to raise us up again. Sometimes we get angry with him along the way. Through receiving Christian care, people who have been estranged from God for a time can experience again how much God still loves and cares for them. We forsake him; but he does not forsake us. As we come alive to our Lord and his will for us, our lives are revitalized and our faith rejuvenated.

Christian Hope

Christian hope is both in the present and for the future. The source of Christian hope is the knowledge that Jesus is with each Christian "yesterday, today, and forever." The person who has received Christian care might display deep-hearted trust in Christ's continuing presence and his return by positive attitudes and expectations.

Christ-Centered Stability

When you base your life on Jesus Christ, you have a firmer foundation than any other. As a favorite hymn declares, "On Christ the solid rock I stand. All other ground is sinking sand," Christ alone is the foundation for holistic stability in your life.

Christ-Centered Self-Image

When the person with whom you are joined in Christian caring truly believes that he or she is a child of God and a temple of the Holy Spirit, that person is going to have a much healthier ego and a realistic self-image. This is not haughtiness or conceit; it is a good feeling about oneself because Jesus Christ is alive and well within.

Peace

As a result of Christian care, a person might come to experience peace. Such peace is not merely the absence of hostility or a state of inner contentment; rather, it is the peace connoted by the Hebrew word *shalom*. As people experience Christian peace, their relationships become whole and complete—with others, with God, and with themselves.

Perspective on Results

This list certainly does not include every distinctively Christian result. Nor does it include all those results of caring that are important, but are not specifically Christian in character—for example, the ability to express one's feelings, greater honesty with oneself and others, overcoming depression, or reducing one's anxiety level.

Another result of Christian caregiving accrues to *you the caregiver*, and it has to do with the strengthening of your own personal faith and Christian life. The more you use the tools of your trade, the better you get, especially when you consider that use implies keeping them in good repair.

Results are great, but they belong to God, who chooses to let you share in the pleasure of them. Don't stalk them; let God send them to you. Desire them, but don't lust after them. Expect results, but don't concentrate on them. Celebrate them, but don't cerebrate them. Be glad when they come, but don't spend a lot of time trying to figure out how to make them come. Count on the certainty that the Lord's sense of timing and purpose is better than yours and better than that of the care receiver. Rely on the promise of the Lord in Rev. 21:5: "I make all things new." Now that's what I call results!

19

Hope-Full Caregiving

One of the most distinctively Christian resources yet to be considered is hope. Part of the unique nature of Christian hope lies in its origin. The responsibility for Christian hope is not yours, but God's. Paul speaks of unbelievers as "having no hope and without God in the world" (Eph. 2:12). Our hope is intimately bound up with God. To have hope solely in human capacities is to despair. Neither you nor I can fix the mess we're in as imperfect human beings in an imperfect world. So, one distinctive aspect of Christian hope is that it comes from and rests securely in God.

Another feature of Christian hope is that it defies the natural. Christian hope is both now and in the future. It is both of these at once, and so our reasoning breaks down when we consider it. This is clearly demonstrated in Jesus' raising of Lazarus:

Jesus said, "Take away the stone." Martha, the sister of the dead man, said to him, "Lord, by this time there will be an odor, for he has been dead four days." Jesus said to her, "Did I not tell you that if you would believe you would see the glory of God?" So they took away the stone. And Jesus lifted up his eyes and said, "Father, I thank thee that thou hast heard me. I know that thou hearest me always, but I have said this on account of the people standing by, that they may believe that thou didst send me.'' When he had said this, he cried with a loud voice, ''Lazarus, come out.'' The dead man came out (John 11:39-44).

Note carefully the tenses of Jesus' prayer. They seem to be reversed. They indicate that as far as Jesus was concerned, Lazarus was already alive. Jesus, who perfectly lived in God-given hope, did not separate the future from the present.

This has dynamic implications for you in your Christian caring. You will bring to your caring the conviction that there is One greater than either you or the problem. This greater One is working through you to produce the same convictions and hope in the care receiver. The Lord of the cosmos is active through your caring. The care receiver is also assured of the now and not yet of his or her hope. Failures will come. Setbacks and disappointments will be present. But in the ''nowness'' of the hope God works, you and the care receiver will be able to look at these and proclaim, ''Not yet!'' You will grow accustomed to seeing things through the hope-inspired glasses of the end of all things as they converge and consummate in Jesus Christ.

As a distinctively Christian caregiver, you can become a facilitator of God's hope. Here are nine practical ways you can become an instrument through which distinctively Christian hope can flow into others.

Sticking with Them

A potent way in which hope manifests itself is when you as a caregiver let people know by your words and actions that you are willing to help them struggle through their problems. Your consistent, caring presence with them through thick and thin instills hope. The knowledge and expectation that another person will be with them during difficult times provides people with a feeling of security.

Being Available

Hope is fostered by letting people know they can get in touch with you any time they need you, especially in an emergency. It is reassuring to another to know that there is someone available around the clock. You might run into situations when people abuse this privilege, but rather than try to circumscribe your caring relationship with qualifiers in advance, it would be better to deal with problems gently and firmly when and if they do arise.

Reducing Anxiety

Often those for whom you care will have a great deal of anxiety. The very act of meeting with you a time or two can serve to reduce the anxiety of the care receiver. A problem shared is a problem halved. Anxiety reduction can be very hope-producing itself.

Sharing the Stories of Others

Sometimes hopelessness comes about because people believe their problems are totally unique. They think their problems are insurmountable because only *they* have experienced them. Sometimes it can be a potent force for hope to share instances you know about in which others have met these same kinds of crises. For example, you might say:

> You don't see how you're going to be able to go on by yourself since your wife died. I've known other husbands

whose wives have died, and they too said how difficult it was at first to be alone.

Or, you might wish to tell them about similar struggles that you yourself have had. For example:

You said you were experiencing some doubts about your faith in God recently. Although right now I feel confident about my relationship with God, a few years ago I too experienced a period of doubt. I would be very happy to listen to your concerns about your faith and maybe later on tell you a few things about myself.

If you choose to share what you or others have experienced, be very careful how you say it. Don't minimize or dismiss the uniqueness of the other's problem. The one you are caring for might interpret what you say as "My friend doesn't understand *my* problem" or "My friend just doesn't know how *I* feel" or "I'm not everybody else—I'm me!" Avoid, for example, saying things like:

I know just how you're feeling. I lost my job once too. Don't worry. Just keep looking and something will turn up. It always does. It did for me.

Or:

Don't you worry about having a baby. Women have been delivering children since the beginning of time. Once you get that baby in your arms, everything will be just fine.

When sharing examples of your own life's struggles, be cautiously selective. There is a difference between being open and being unzipped! For example, suppose you are talking to a teenager who has just been caught vandalizing a local school. If you happen to have been guilty of the same offense when you were much younger, it probably would not be a good idea to share this information with the young person. This might serve only to confuse him or her, and create doubts about the wrongness of the behavior.

Areas of similarity that you may appropriately share might include your own feelings of sadness and despondency when someone close to you died; that you too, as a new parent, were extremely frustrated and depressed; that you too felt sad, lonely, and "used up" when your last child went off to college, and so on. There is no ironclad rule about sharing aspects of your personal life with another, whether you are a professional or lay caregiver. Being vulnerable can be helpful, but don't share information that could confuse the other or reduce your credibility. Some things are better left unsaid.

You can encourage considerable hope by sharing that others with similar life situations have successfully worked them through. Here too you need to be careful in what you say:

Don't say: Others have done it this way and you can too.
Do say: I have known others who had similar difficulties. Although it was not easy for them as they struggled through their problems, in doing so they were able to resolve them. I hope that as we deal with these difficulties of yours, the same will be true for you.

Without minimizing the uniqueness of their problems, tactfully impress on those you care for that there is good potential for them to work through their difficulties (if this is indeed the case). Avoid telling success stories about heroic Christians who soared through severe storms of life with flying colors. The person might not feel very heroic and become depressed by making an unfavorable comparison in his or her mind with someone who exhibited tremendous personal resources when dealing with a problem.

Accepting the Other

By communicating through words and actions your acceptance of people despite their problems and faults, you can also instill hope. Unconditional acceptance leads to trust, and trust is closely followed by hope. If a person says, "I hate my mother. I wish she were dead," there are nonaccepting and accepting ways to respond.

Don't say (*gasping with shock*): "That's terrible! You should not say that."

Do say: It sounds like you are angry at your mother. (*Pause*) I'm willing to listen.

By communicating acceptance to others despite their problems and their sins—just as Jesus does with you—you can produce great hope in others.

Emphasizing the Positive

Sometimes individuals feel so broken that they can no longer discover any good in themselves. Natural talents and skills are all but obscured by an exaggerated sense of their problems and negative feelings about themselves. You can instill hope in the person for whom you are caring by emphasizing those positive characteristics. This is precisely what Jesus did when Nathaniel was brought to him. He said, "Behold, an Israelite indeed, in whom is no guile!" (John 1:47). Jesus could have said, "Behold a sinner who needs repentance!" Rather, in this instance he chose to accentuate the positive.

Realizing Failures and Limitations

Discovering the positive includes, by implication, the realization that no one is all positive, that everyone has failures and limitations. Jesus often praised Peter, but did not hesitate to rebuke him publicly when necessary. Knowing who Peter was to become, Jesus spoke the truth in love to him about his forthcoming denial on the eve of the crucifixion. Like bad-tasting medicine, confronting in love the faults and limitations of another can engender hope. The faults and limitations of a care receiver are actually promises that Jesus still has healing to perform. You can take heart that your own weaknesses and failures are opportunities for God's strength to show itself, and you can lovingly communicate the same vision to another.

Jesus with You

What a comfort that Jesus is not only *in* you, but *with* you—with both the caregiver and the care receiver. The Christian condition is not just Jesus inside you, wonderful as that news is. It is the joy of realizing that Jesus is an objective, supportive presence on the outside as well. He is before you to lead you. He is behind you to guard you. He is beside you that he may support and comfort you. He is above you to bless you. In short, he is with and for you!

Being Distinctively Christian

Finally, you can instill hope by simply being distinctively Christian. By speaking in distinctively Christian terms and relating to others in a distinctively Christian manner, you convey your competence as a Christian caregiver, thereby instilling hope. The *language* of hope is one aspect of Christian caregiving. The *fact* of hope is what Christian care aims for.

These practical ways to bring hope to a person in need have a common thread: they ask you to imitate Christ. You stay with the person as Christ stays with you. You are available to the other as Christ is available to you. You reduce the other's anxiety as your union with Christ reduces yours. You lead others back into human community, ending their isolation as Christ ended your isolation from God. You accept the person as Christ accepts you, freeing you from judgment. You accentuate the positive as Christ does for you. You strengthen the other to confront failure and limitation as Christ strengthens you. You are a Christ to the other by your Christian caring.

All this hope-producing power is yours because Jesus Christ is in you, with you, above you, beside you, behind you, and for you.

20

The Thrill of It All

Top-notch caregiving happens in many arenas of action. Excellent physicians mend a host of physical ailments. Competent mental health professionals devote themselves to the healing of mental and emotional distress. Then there's you, equipped with the unique tools of Christian caring and increasingly aware of the distinctive nature of your calling. The unique vantage point you bring to the hurt and broken world makes you very important along with all other healers and helpers. They are doing excellent, necessary work. So are you.

Power and Potential

Remember whose power you bring into every situation— the power of God the Father, his loving Son, and the Holy Spirit.

Remember *what* power you bring to each situation—the Bible, prayer, confession, forgiveness, servanthood, hope, and other distinctively Christian resources.

To me, the power of God and the potential of these resources are thrilling!

● I am comforted that I am not the only one who experiences difficulties in being distinctively Christian.

● I am relieved that my calling is to be a caregiver, while God is the curegiver.

● I feel a sense of partnership and security, knowing that God is fully present with me and the other person in the caring situation.

● I have purpose and direction because I know who motivates me, where I come from, and where I am going.

● I feel more competent because I have tools like prayer, Scripture, and blessings.

● I feel a sense of inner warmth (and sometimes fear and trembling) when I am privileged to relate to people's deep spiritual needs.

● I am free to go the extra mile with those who need me, enhanced by a healthy Christian perspective on servanthood.

● I rejoice that the "cups of cold water" I give to others are accepted by God as distinctively Christian caring.

● I draw courage from the long line of tradition in which my caring stands, realizing that I actively continue the work carried on by God's people throughout the ages.

Integrating Theology and Psychology

Asserting the need for unique and distinctive Christian caregiving is what I've been doing throughout this book. I would like to share with you a little more of my own background so that you can better understand my preoccupation with the theme. My education was neatly split. I went to a Christian grade school, high school, college, and seminary. At the end of that, I was pronounced fit and ready to be a pastor. In addition to my theological training, I acquired a Ph.D. in clinical psychology, which was for the most part "secular" education and training. At the end of four years I was pronounced fit and ready to be a psychologist.

What I wasn't prepared for was to integrate the two. But integration is what I believe is most sorely needed. Because my psychological training was almost totally secular, I think I have developed an even greater appreciation for the power and possibilities of the spiritual combined with the science and practice of psychology. Psychology and the health sciences make substantial contributions to the well-being of people. So does theology. When the two are wedded in a practical and healthy union, the possibilities are boundless.

In this book, my intent has been to take you beyond theorizing about the integration of psychology and theology. Christianity is, above all, practical. Its exercise, benefits, and demands begin not in the sweet by-and-by, but here and now. What I hope you have received from me is confidence, inspiration, and excitement about *your* potential for unique and distinctive caring as a Christian, with the insights of psychology and theology wedded inside you.

Your Caregiving Journey

Now is the time for action, and in that sense I am "seeing you off at the station." Your journey will be the result of God's call and your own distinctive gifts. I am excited to have been a part of your journey thus far. I am thrilled and expectant for what the rest of your journey will bring. My prayer is that you have found in this book an empowering resource for being distinctively Christian in any caregiving that you do.

May the peace and joy of almighty God the Father, Son, and Holy Spirit go with you.

About the Author

Rev. Kenneth C. Haugk, Ph.D., a pastor and clinical psychologist, is the founder and executive director of Stephen Ministries St. Louis.

As a parish pastor in 1975, he discovered that the needs for care in his congregation exceeded what he alone could provide, so he drew on his psychological and theological background to train nine members as Stephen Ministers to work with him in providing care to members of the congregation and community. With the great success of that first Stephen Ministry and with the strong encouragement of two of the Stephen Ministers, Dr. Haugk and his wife Joan founded Stephen Ministries to bring caring ministry to other congregations. Since then, more than 11,000 congregations and other organizations have started Stephen Ministry and more than a half-million Stephen Ministers have been trained.

Joan's death from ovarian cancer in 2002 deepened his passion for Christian caregiving—and has resulted in several more books, including *Don't Sing Songs to a Heavy Heart* and *Journeying through Grief.*

In addition to leading the efforts of the staff at the Stephen Ministries Center in St. Louis, Dr. Haugk likes to play basketball, fish, travel, and spend time with his family.

Dr. Haugk has received numerous awards, including the National Samaritan Award from the Samaritan Institute for significant contributions to the field of caring ministry. He is a frequent keynote speaker at conferences on Christian caregiving, grief, spiritual gifts, church antagonism, leadership, and other topics.

Stephen Ministries

Stephen Ministries is a not-for-profit Christian training and educational organization founded in 1975 and based in St. Louis, Missouri. Its mission is:

> To equip the saints for the work of ministry, for building up the body of Christ, until all of us come to the unity of the faith and of the knowledge of the Son of God, to maturity, to the measure of the full stature of Christ.
>
> *Ephesians 4:12–13*

The 40-person staff of Stephen Ministries carries out this mission by developing and delivering high-quality, Christ-centered training and resources to:

- help congregations and other organizations equip and organize people to do meaningful ministry; and
- help individuals grow spiritually, relate and care more effectively, and live out their faith in daily life.

Stephen Ministries is best known for the Stephen Series system of lay caring ministry, but it also offers resources in many other areas, including grief support, assertiveness, spiritual gifts, ministry mobilization, caring evangelism, church antagonism, and inactive member ministry.

A number of these resources are described on the following pages. To learn more about these and other resources or to order them, contact us at:

Stephen Ministries
2045 Innerbelt Business Center Drive
St. Louis, Missouri 63114-5765
(314) 428-2600
www.stephenministries.org

The Stephen Series

 The Stephen Series is a complete system for training and organizing laypeople to provide one-to-one Christian care to hurting people in the congregation and community.

Stephen Leaders—pastors, staff, and lay leaders—are trained to begin and lead Stephen Ministry in the congregation.

Stephen Leaders, in turn, equip and supervise a team of Stephen Ministers—congregation members who provide ongoing care and support to people experiencing grief, divorce, hospitalization, terminal illness, unemployment, loneliness, and other life difficulties.

As a result:

- hurting people receive quality care during times of need;
- laypeople use their gifts in meaningful ministry;
- pastors no longer are expected to personally provide all the care that people need; and
- the congregation grows as a more caring community.

More than 11,000 congregations and organizations from more than 150 denominations—from across the United States, Canada, and 24 other countries—have enrolled in the Stephen Series so they can more effectively provide Christ-centered care to people in need.

Christian Caregiving—a Way of Life is one of the books Stephen Ministers read during their initial training.

Journeying through Grief

Journeying through Grief is a set of four short books that individuals, congregations, and other organizations can share with grieving people at  four crucial times during the first year after a loved one has died.

Book 1: *A Time to Grieve,* sent three weeks after the loss

Book 2: *Experiencing Grief,* sent three months after the loss

Book 3: *Finding Hope and Healing,* sent six months after the loss

Book 4: *Rebuilding and Remembering,* sent eleven months after the loss

Each book focuses on the feelings and issues the person is likely to be experiencing at that point in their grief, offering reassurance, encouragement, and hope. In *Journeying through Grief,* Kenneth Haugk writes in a warm, caring style. He shares from the heart, drawing on his personal and professional experience and from the insights of many others. The books provide a simple yet powerful way to express ongoing concern to a bereaved person throughout the difficult first year.

Each set comes with four mailing envelopes and a tracking card that makes it easy to know when to send each book.

Also available is a *Giver's Guide* containing suggestions for using the books as well as sample letters that can be personalized and adapted to send with them.

Don't Sing Songs to a Heavy Heart: How to Relate to Those Who Are Suffering

Pastors, lay caregivers, and suffering people alike have high praise for *Don't Sing Songs to a Heavy Heart* by Kenneth Haugk, a warm and practical resource for what to do and say to hurting people in times of need.

Forged in the crucible of Dr. Haugk's own suffering and grief, *Don't Sing Songs to a Heavy Heart* draws from his personal experience and from extensive research with more than 4,000 other people.

For anyone who has ever felt helpless in the face of another person's pain, *Don't Sing Songs to a Heavy Heart* offers practical guidance and common-sense suggestions for how to care in ways that hurting people welcome—while avoiding the pitfalls that can add to their pain.

With its combination of sound psychology and solid biblical truths, *Don't Sing Songs to a Heavy Heart* provides a wonderful follow-up to *Christian Caregiving—a Way of Life.*